Abstracts
of
Oder Book "O"
Patrick County
Virginia

- 1791-1800 -

Compiled by:
Lela C. Adams

Southern Historical Press, Inc.
Greenville, South Carolina

Please direct all correspondence and orders to:

www.southernhistoricalpress.com
or
SOUTHERN HISTORICAL PRESS, Inc.
PO BOX 1267
Greenville, SC 29601
southernhistoricalpress@gmail.com

ISBN #0-89308-427-1

Printed in the United States of America

PREFACE

The Court Order Books have been considered by many genealogists and historians as the most useful single document for research. They include: administration and inventory of estates, deed acknowledgments, bills of sale, deeds of gift, leases, powers of attorney, appointments of militia officers, Consitutional officers of the County, lists of the establishments of roads, mills, ordinaries as well as the day-to-day record of the County. The early Patrick County Order Books have not been indexed, making their use limited.

You will note the first Court is recorded as 13 June 1791 on Page 1, the next entry being 11 June 1792. The original book has several blank pages after the first entry, leading one to think they were left blank to be filled in at a later date.

The names listed are as interpreted, and there are various spellings listed for the same individual, for example: Mabry, Mayberry, Maybury. Perigo, Peregoy, Pedigo. Rhodham Moore is listed as Rhoda and Roda Moore. Nowlin, Nowlen, Nolen. The spellings of words are listed as written.

PLEASE NOTE THIS CONCERNING PAGE NUMBERS FOUND IN THE INDEX: The page numbers of individuals listed in the Index are the page numbers of the original Court Order Book and are found at the left side of every page of this book,..and they are underlined for your convenience. Please do NOT refer to the page numbers at the bottom of each page when trying to find particular individuals.

Compiled by
Lela C. Adams
Bassett, Virginia

PATRICK COUNTY, VIRGINIA
ORDER BOOK "O" 1791-1800

Page 1

-At the Courthouse of Patrick County on Monday 13 June 1791, a Commissioner of the Peace from his Excellency the Governor dated at Richmond 14 May 1791 last directed to Abraham Penn, gentleman, and others was produced and read. By virtue whereof the Abraham Penn administered the oath of a Justice of the Peace the oath of Justice in Chancery and oath of Oyer. Oaths to: Jonathan Hanby, Daniel Carlin, Samuel Clark, William Carter, Stephen Lyon, Francis Turner, James Armstrong, William Banks and Charles Foster.
-William Mitchell, gentleman, produced a commission from his Excellency the Governor appointing him Sherif of Patrick County and took the usual oaths with George Hairston, Abraham Penn and James Armstrong his security.
-Samuel Staples is appointed Clerk of this Court with security: William Banks, William Carter, James Poteet and James Taylor.
-On the motion of Samuel Staples, Clerk, John Cox is appointed his Deputy.
-John Call, gentleman, is recommended to the Attorney General as a fit person to serve as Deputy States Attorney for this County.
-Brett Stovall is recommended to the Masters of William and Mary Colledge as a fit and proper person to serve as Surveyor for the County.

Page 2

-James Charles sworn as Constable
-John Call, gentleman, qualified as attorney at law
-Deed- Samuel Street to Ralph Danger
-Deed- same to Anthony Collings
-Deed- same to Thomas Collings
-On the motion of William Mitchell sheriff, Thomas Mitchell is admitted as deputy sheriff.
-Court adjourned till tomorrow at 10 o'clock. A. Penn
-Court, Tuesday 14 June 1791, present: Abraham Penn, James Lyon, Jonathan Hanby, Daniel Carlin, Samuel Clark, William Carter, Stephen Lyon, James Armstrong, Francis Turner, William Banks, Charles Foster.
-George Poor Jr is appointed surveyor of the road from Patrick County line to Fee's Meadow, list filed.

Page 3

-Court 11 June 1792 present: Abram Penn, James Lyon, William Banks, Samuel Clark
-A report of a view of the road from the Chestnut Hollow opposite George Rogers to the North Carolina line at Harts Rd returned.
-James Slator is appointed surveyor of the road from the mouth of Penns line to the Henry line below old Harris' in the room of Joseph Morrison.
-William Buckley, John Ward, Richard Hopkins are added to Peter Frances list of hands. John France and William Stone are discharged.
-Humphrey Smith is appointed surveyor of the road from Coxs Road to Daniel Ross in place of Bond? Burnett.
-Charles Ferrell is appointed surveyor of the road from Bull Mountain into River Road near Foleys in place of John Hancock.
-George Carter and John Nunn came into Court to qualify as Overseers of the Poor for this County.
-James Thompson is exempt from the payment of County and Parish levies during his infirmity.
-Alexander Frazor is appointed Constable in place of Aquilla Blackley.
-David Rogers is appointed to open and clear a road view from the Chestnut Hollow opposite George Rogers to the North Carolina line at Harts Road.
-Wilson & Co. vs Shelton
-Brooks vs Cloud
-same vs same - Miller Easley, Spl Bl
-Edward Lewis an invalid pensioner of this state, came into Court,

said Court is of the opinion that he should be reinstated and his pay continued.
-Ordered that the Sheriff pay Edward Lewis fifteen pounds out of his collection for 1791.

Page 4

-Ordered that James Lyon be added to the Commission appointed to superintend the laying off and selling the lots in the town at this Courthouse.
-Goings vs Eckolds
-Boyd vs Doak
-Lyon vs Gains
-Lyon vs Sawyers
-Rowark vs Johnson
-Ordered that Lewis Johnson be summoned to appear at next Court and give an account of his breach of office as Constable.
-Samuel Clark, William Banks and Stephen Lyon appointed to settle the current account with the Administrator of Henry Parr, dec'd, report.
-James Lyon, William Banks, Stephen Lyon, William Carter and Samuel Clark appointed to inspect the County Jail and report.
-Stephen Lyon came into Court and produced a Commission appointing him Major in the Militia.
-Samuel Staples same as Captain of the Militia
-Leander Hughes qualified as Ensign of Infantry; John Parr Jr as Lt of Militia.
-Shelton vs McDonald, Stephen Lyon a garnishee being sworn that he owes the defendant 11 yds of gause and 5 womens hats.
-Lyon vs Hunter
-Ordered the Sheriff pay Samuel Staples 40 shillings for a record book furnished the Surveyor of the County.

Page 5

Court July 9, 1792 present: James Armstrong, Charles Foster, William Banks, Francis Turner, William Carter.
-Goings vs Ackolds (Echols)
-Lyon vs Gaines
-Rowark vs Johnson
-Corn vs France
-Philpott vs France
-Boyd vs Doak
-Lyons vs Sawyers
-Johnson vs Rowark
-Shelton vs McDonald
-Deed- Standwix Hord and John Hord to John Redd. Ruth Hord, wife of John Hord relinquishes her right of dower.
-Joseph France is appointed surveyor of the road from Dry Pond to the Widow Easleys.
-On the motion of William Mitchell sheriff, William Lindsay is admitted as his Deputy.
-A report of a view of a road from the Dry Pond to Widow Easleys returned.
-Deed- James Taylor to William Smith Sr, George Carter, John Medley Sr, James Taylor, Joseph Cummings and David Taylor.
-John Tuggle appointed surveyor of the road from George Mabrays to the top of the mountain in place of George Mabry.
-James Denny appointed surveyor of the road from the fork of the road below the Widow Lackeys to George Mabrys in place of George Mabry.
-Account current of John Parr Jr administrator of Henry Parr dec'd retd.
-David McGown is discontinued as surveyor of the road, Jacob Johnson appointed.

Page 6

-Deed- David Rogers to Mary Thomas
-Brooks vs Cloud, Nathaniel Smith security
-James Lyon is appointed County Treasurer
-William Banks, Samuel Clark, William Carter and James Lyon are appointed to view a way for a road from the east end of the low cross street into the road that leads by Eliphaz Shelton and report.
-Report: to alter the upper cross street and extend those streets not already extended. A report of a view of a road from the east end of the lower cross street into the road that leads to Eliphaz Sheltons.

Pg 6 contd
-Ordered that John Sharp and his gang clear a road from Main Street to the outside of Town and from thence into the road that leads by Eliphaz Shelton so as to strike the road 20 yards below a kind of punchen bridge about 120 y ards from the east end.
-Ordered that Charles Ferrell call on Humphrey Smith and James Poteet Jr and their hands to clear and open a road from Corns Road near Harbers Shop into the new road that leads from Bartlett Foley to Daniel Ross at Samuel Noe's plantation.
-A report of a view of a road from Patrick County to John Nunns.
-Edward Tatum came into Court and qualified his list of taxable property.
-James Rea came into Court and produced credentials of his being in regular communion with the Baptist Society.
-William Mitchell, Daniel Carlin and Samuel Clark are recommended to the Governor as proper persons to serve as Sheriff of the County.
-Ordered that David Lawson, Randal Lawson, Andrew Polson and Robert Bowman be summoned to give testamony against Lewis Johnson on account of his breach of office.
-Edward Tatum is allowed 67 days for his service in taking a list of taxable property for the year 1792.

PAGE 7

August quarter session 1792
-William Mitchell sheriff, came into Court with James Lyon, Samuel Clark his security and entered into Bond for the collection of the County Levey for the year 1791.
Court 13 August 1792 present: James Lyon, James Armstrong, Francis Turner, Samuel Clark, William Carter.
-William Headspeth qualified as Overseer of the Poor
-Thomas Stone is exempt from payment of County and parish levies for the future.
-Jury: Augustine Thomas foreman, William McAlexander, Henry McGuffey, William Sharp, John Henderson, Jacob Adams Jr, William Smith Jr, Isaac Adams, Hamon France, James Taylor, George Penn, William Witt, Samuel Perry, James Poteet Jr, William Handcock, Samuel Kennon, Munford Smith and William Griffin.
-Adams vs Price, George Hairston admitted as arbitrator in place of James Baker.
-James Dabney gentleman produced license to practice law in this and other inferior courts.
-Gardner vs Barker
-Hunter vs Pulliam
-Brooks vs Cloud, Pltf to take depo of Robert Kyle, Samuel Wilson, Thomas Brooks, Stokley Donelson.
-Murrell vs Tuggle, John Tuggle Spl Bl

PAGE 8

August Court 1792 present: Abraham Penn, James Lyon, Samuel Clark, Stephen Lyon, Francis Turner, Jonathan Hanby, William Carter, Charles Foster, James Armstrong.
-Archelaus Hughes tooks oaths and is considered Presiding Judge of this Court.
-Bolling vs Lyon, jury sworn: Humphrey Smith, Obadiah Hudson, James Dickerson, William Barton, Henry Smith, William Gardner, Henry Tuggle, Josiah Briant, Jeremiah Burnett, Jesse Tatum, George Brooks, George Mabray..jury disagreed.
-John France qualified as Lt of a company of light infantry.
-James Varnell produced license to practice law.
-Gossett vs Lawson, referred to James Lyon, William Carter, Jonathan Hanby.
-Lyne vs King, Holden McGhee Spl Bl
-William B. Price qualified as Ensign of Militia
-Samuel Allen exempt from the payment of County and parish levies for the future.

PAGE 9

Present: Archelaus Hughes, James Lyon, Samuel Clark, Francis Turner and William Carter.
-Lyon vs Amoss, jury sworn: Humphrey Smith, Edward Lewis, William Barton, Henry Smith, Jesse Tatum, John Henderson, David Rowark, William Keaton, Humberston Lyon, William Cloud, George Brooks, George Mabray. Verdict for the Pltf.
-Koger vs Shelton - contd
-Laurance vs Dickerson - contd
-Johnson vs Allen, jury sworn (same as above) verdict for Pltf.
-Laurance vs Dickerson, Pltf to take depo of Hugh Armstrong, Elijah Smallwood and David Apling.
-Keaton vs Barker, Def confessed judgment, granted stay of 1 month.
-Mankin vs King, contd
-Stewart vs Hunter, dism.
-Mankin vs King, Def. to take depo of David Dose.
-Rickman vs B. Kennon, jury sworn: George Carter, Adam Turner, John Hawks, William Woody, Joseph Reynolds, Samuel Shelton, Henry Tuggle, Thomas Hornsby, Joseph Laurance, James Ferrell, Henry Koger, Brett Stovall. Verdict retd for Pltf.
-Irby vs Lewis, defendant confessed judgment
-Ordered the the Surveyor of the County lay off 10 acres of ground for the Prison bounds, including the Prison, Courthouse and Ordinary and that Abraham Penn and William Carter superintend the laying off and report to the Court.
-Mabray vs Kinzey, referred to Thomas Garrison, Henry Tuggle, William Isham and this to be the judgment of the Court.

PAGE 10

-George Corn is alld 4 days witn. for William Rickman
-Isaac Hollandsworth 10 days for same
-Bartlett Reynolds same
-The Committee appointed to receive the County Jail reported it is done according to contract.
-William Mitchell came into Court and objected to the sufficiency of the Jail.
-Salsberry vs Gea
-Willis vs Sharp, defendant confessed judgment
-Sheriff to pay Abram Penn forty pounds in part for building the Prison
-Saunders assignee vs Poteet Jr, judgment for Pltf
-Lyon vs Gains, contd
-William vs Litteral, dismd
-On a motion of Samuel Allen by John Dabney gentleman, his attorney an injunction is granted him to stay the proceedings of a judgment obtained by John Johnson against him on his giving bond and security in the Clerks office in 20 days.
-Tatum & Co vs Mankin, judgment for Pltf
-Goings vs Ackolds, dismd
-Commonwealth vs Barrott, judgment
- same vs Francis, dismissed
- same vs Kinzey "
- same vs Burnett Jr ""
-same vs Hawks contd
- same vs Hoof contd
-same vs Smith contd
- same vs Elliott dism
- same vs Hollandsworth, judgment
- same vs Cooper, judgment
-On a motion of Eliphaz Shelton's complaining of a road from the Courthouse into a road near Shadrack Barretts.
-Lewis Johnson discontinued as Constable and Amos Rowark appointed in his place.

Page 11

September Court 1792 present: James Lyon, William Banks, Samuel Clark, William Carter.

Pg 11 contd

-Adams vs Price, judgment for Pltf
-Critz vs Mankin, dism
Present: A. Hughes, Francis Turner
-Lyon vs Gains
-William Banks and Jacob Critz are appointed Trustees for Coonrad Bush who is looked upon by this Court as an object of Charity.
-Deed- Thomas Henderson to William Pilson
-On a motion of Stephen Lyon judgment is granted him against John Smith for the administration of a judgment obtained by Eliphaz Shelton, executor of Ralph Shelton as security for said Smith.
-George Carter made oath that Parish Simms is heir at law of James Sims deceased.
-Rentfro vs Hoof
-Smith vs Maynor
-Read vs Going
-Hairston vs Hooker
-Ordered that George Carter call John Sharp and his hands and George Stults and his, Carter with his and clear and open a road viewed from the Courthouse to John Nunns on Little Dan.
-Samuel Corn, Peter Corn, John Parr Jr, John Parr Sr or any 3 to view a way for a road from where Samuel Corns path leaves the Hollow Road into Hughes Road.
-Thomas Gee and Mathew Small came into Court and acknowledged debt to the Commonwealth..condition that Gee be of good behaviour one year and one day towards Richard Salisbury.
-Rickman vs Koger

PAGE 12

-Sim vs Going, David Going Spl Bl
-William Banks gentleman, allowed 30 pounds for 5 days attendance as a Commissioner attending and selling the lots for the use of the County. Samuel Clark 7 days for same; William Carter 7 days for same; Charles Foster 4 days for same.
-Court 8 October 1792 present: James Lyon, William Banks, Samuel Clark, Stephen Lyon.
-Dickerson vs Laurance, Def. to take depo of William Hammonds, William Falkner, John Hammonds Jr, John Breson Jr, Stephen J.K. Smith, Mallory Smith.
-Hord vs Sharp
-Gabriel Penn is permitted to clear the Courthouse lot for the use of the timber, reserving a few trees for shade or as the Commissioners may choose.
-Rickman vs J. Kennon
-On a motion of Sherod Stephens by John W. Hunter his attorney, an injunction is granted him to stay the proceedings of a judgment obtained against him by Edward Tatum until the same can be heard in equity and together with William Bolling his security entered into Bond.
-Lyon vs Gains
-Farrell vs Tatum
-Smith vs Sarah Joneson

PAGE 13

-Perkins Jr vs Blackley
-Overseers of the Poor bind out Thomas Parr, John Parr, Nancy Parr and Miriam Parr poor orphans according to Law.
-Saunders assignee vs Breden Jr
-Read vs Going
-Ordered that the Commissioners previously appointed to settle with Henry County the depositium in the Sheriff's hands, settle and receive whatsoever sum they may be entitled to.
-Report of a view of the road from Samuel Corns path, Hollow Road, Hughes Road. Ordered that Peter Corn to call on John Parr Jr and his hands, George Poor Jr and his to clear said road.

Page 13 contd

Monday 17 November 1792 present: James Lyon, Jonathan Hanby, William Banks, Francis Turner
-Deed- George Walton to ..France
-Deed- same to Peter Scales
-Last Will and Testament of William Bristoe exhibited and proved by one witness.

PAGE 14

Tuesday 13 November 1792 present: A. Hughes, James Lyon, William Banks, Francis Turner, Samuel Clark

-Deed- John Cammeron to John Renn
-On a motion of John Koger leave is granted him to keep an ordinary at this Courthouse with Samuel Staples his security.
-Hall vs Amoss, James Morrison Spl Bl and delivered him up into the custody of William Perkins Jr.
-Commonwealth vs Johnson
-same vs Poteet, Jr
-same vs Saunders
-Lyon vs Gains
-Mankin vs Boaham
-Perkins Jr vs Blackley
-Read vs Going
-Saunders assignee vs Braden Jr
-Sublett vs Henderson
-Terrell vs Tatum
-Salsberry vs Branham
-Henderson assignee vs Hammons
-Detheridge vs Penn
-Mabray Sr assignee vs M. Barker
-Ellison vs Rickman
-Hughes & Hairston vs Scott
-Bolling vs Cloud, jury sworn: William Perkins Sr, William Amos, David Rogers, Humphrey Smith, John Crum, Moses Walden, Thomas Ward, Hamon France, Woody Burge, Joseph Reynolds, Jeremiah Burnett, James Baker. Verdict retd for Pltf, defendant appeals.
-Shelton vs Mankin, on a Atta. Henry Harrison Dean a garnishee being served owes defendant 2 saddles and 3 flax wheels.
-Garrott vs Lawson
-Hughes vs Smith

Page 15

-Laurance vs Dickerson, jury sworn: John Breden Sr, Tandy Senter, John Wright, Laurance Lee, George Brooks, David Harber, Elisha Harber, Samuel Dalton, William Cloud, Henry H. Deen, Humberston Lyon, Robert Hedspeath. Verdict retd each party to pay own cost.
-Turner vs Henderson
-Deberaux Gilliam alld 3 days 18 miles witness George Brooks vs William Cloud
-Jacob Lawson 6 days for same
-W. Keaton vs W. Adams
-Going vs Rickman
-Sims vs David Going
-James Baker alld 1 day 25 miles witness Henry Lyne vs Joseph King
-C. Keaton vs Adams
-Mankin vs King
-John Tatum is admitted as under-sheriff of the County

Patrick County	Dr. pounds of Tobacco
Clerk for annual salary	1248.
Sherif same	1248.
Deputy State Attorney	1248.
	3744.

Court adjourned

PAGE 16

Monday 10 December 1792 present: Abraham Penn, James Lyon, William Banks, William Carter

-Deed-John Marr to Shadrick Going
-Mabray Jr vs Kimzey, award retd for Pltf for 33-½ gallons good marketable brandy and cost
-Deed- Andrew Herran to John Simmon
-Read vs Going
-Ellison vs Rickman
-Price vs Walden
-Fletcher vs Commins
-Copley vs Rickman
-Copley vs Shelton
-Edward Tatum is appointed surveyor of the road in place of Woody Burge, list filed.
-George Mabry Jr is appointed surveyor of the road from Francis Turners to the Mountain in place of Richard Pilson.
-Adam Turner appointed surveyor of the road from Francis Turners to Foleys in room of Richard Pilson
-Corn vs Adams
-Eliphaz Shelton appointed surveyor of the road from this Courthouse into Carters Road near the Wolf Pitts and to keep in repair.

-County Levy for Year 1792 brt fwd	3744.
-to Obadiah Hudson for 1 old wolfs head	100.
	3844.

PAGE 17

Court Monday 10 January 1793 present: Abram Penn, James Lyon, Francis Turner, Samuel Clark
-Keaton vs Simmons and wife
-Bill of sale from Stephen Lyon to Humberston Lyon and Miller Easley
-Deed- Joseph Cummings to Harris Carter
-Deed- Abraham E. Rowden to Isham Cradock
-William Fain appointed surveyor of the road in place of William Barton
-Deed- William Wood to John Eadins, Jane Wood, wife of William Wood, relinquished her right of dower.
-Deed-Jesse Simmons and Milley Simmons his wife to Joseph Keaton
-Deed- Joseph Keaton to Henry Parr deceased orphans
-Read vs Going
-Detheridge vs Penn
-Tatum vs Shelton
-Lackey vs Tuggle
-On a motion of Edward Lewis invalid pension of this State, the Sherif to pay him 30 pounds out of the 1791 collection.
-William Mitchell sheriff came into Court with Abram Penn and Samuel Clark his security for collecting revenue tax for year 1792.
-Barrott vs Simmon

PAGE 18

The County levy for 1792 brt fwd	3844.
to James Denny for Benjamin Kimzey, one old wolf head	100.
to Samuel Staples for Benjamin Garett same	100.
to Eliphaz Shelton for A. Ward, 2 days attending surveyor	40.
to Eliphaz Shelton for Miles Barrett same	40.
	4124.

Court Monday 14 January 1793 present: Abram Penn, James Lyon, Samuel Clark, William Banks, Francis Turner.
-Thomas and Job Gee brought into Court on suspicion of breaking open the house of Benjamin Kimzey and taking out a quantity of brandy. Said Thomas and Job Gee lead to the Bar in custody of William Mitchell pleaded not guilty, the Court examined them and are of the opinion they are not guilty.

PAGE 19

Court Monday 11 February 1793 present: James Lyon, William Banks, William Carter, Jonathan Hanby.

-Deed- Hamon Frans to Peter Frans
-Adams Rowark qualified as Constable
-Francis Turner, Jesse Corn, Beveridge Hughes and Thomas Morrow or any 3, to view a way for a road from the top of Abner Ridge into the same road a short distance from beyond William Hancocks.
-Benjamin Mize is appointed surveyor of the road in place of William Bristoe from Charles Fosters to the Franklin line.
-John Gossett appointed surveyor of the road in place of John Witt from the top of Bull Mountain to the Henry line.
-On the motion of Brett Stovall, Joseph Martin is admitted as Deputy Surveyor, and it is ordered that he be examined touching his capacity by the Surveyor of Henry County.
-David Lawson, Thomas Lawson, Joel Morris, Jacob Lawson and George Rogers came into Court. David Lawson, Thomas Lawson and Joel Morris are to be of good behaviour to the citizens of the Commonwealth and especially towards Benjamin Garrett for 12 months 1 day.
-Lackey vs Tuggle, referred to Francis Turner & David Robertson
-Read vs Going
-Lackey vs Tuggle
-Frazor vs Berry
-King vs McGhee
-Barnard vs Smith
-Price vs Walden
-Copley vs Fletcher
-Hambleton vs Rick
-Hairston vs Tittle
-Burns ? vs Jones
-Bolt vs Small
-Koger vs Warden Jr
-An inquisition on the body of Francis Barrett returned

PAGE 20

The County levy for the year 1792 fwd	4124.
to Brett Stovall for laying off lots in town of Taylorsville	820.
to Charles Foster for Charles Dalton Jr 1 old wolf head	100.
to Thomas Mitchell for Christopher Roles, 10 young and 1 old wolf head	600.
to same for called Court and examination of Jesse Reynolds	300.
to same for Thomas and Job Gee	600.
to Edward Tatum for Roderick Shelton,wolf head	100.
to Clerk for Called Court & examine Jesse Reynolds	200.
to same for Job and Thomas Gee	600.
to same, service to Commonwealth	1500.
to a depositium for County use	2386.
to Sherif for collecting	770.
by 1,000 tithables @ 12 pounds tobacco per poll	12000.

PAGE 21

Monday 11 March 1793 present: James Lyon, Charles Foster, Samuel Clark, William Carter.

-Deed- Samuel Hairston to Samuel Posey
-Jury: James Taylor foreman, William Isam, James Elkins, Sharp Barton, William Fuson, William Easley, William Burnett, William Hancock, George Rogers, John Burnett, Samuel Kennon, George Rogers Jr, William Branham Jr, Benjamin Hancock, Elisha Harbour, Moses Walden, Joseph Street are sworn as Grand Jury of inquest for the body of this Court and returned to consider presentments.

Page 21 contd

-Edward Henry, gentleman, produced license to practice law in the inferior courts of the Commonwealth.
-Joseph Martin qualified as Deputy Surveyor under Brett Stovall
-Edward Tatum appointed Coroner with Jonath Hanby and Nathaniel Smith is security.
-Hall vs Amos, referred to Charles Foster, Edward Tatum, John Hancock and Richard Pilson
-Amos vs Hall referred to same
-Mayberry vs Branham, referred to Francis Turner, Jeremiah Burnett Jr, David Morgan and Jesse Corn
-Commonwealth vs Branham, dismissed at Cost

PAGE 22

Court Tuesday 12 March 1793 present: Abram Penn, James Armstrong, James Lyon, Charles Foster, Samuel Clark, Francis Turner, William Carter

-Commonwealth vs Sundrys
-Robert Wilson, by his attorney vs B. Philpott
-Read vs Going
-Lackey vs Tuggle
-Frazor vs Berry
-King vs McGee
-Barnard vs Smith
-Price vs Walden
-Copley vs Voss and Fletcher
-Hairston vs Tittle
-Barm..? vs Jones
-Bolt vs Samuel
-Koger vs Warden
-Edward Tatum vs Webb
-Adams vs Mankin & Keaton, Jacob Adams Spl Bl for Keaton
-Bouldin vs Lyon, jury sworn: Martin Amoss, Nathan Hall, Humphrey Smith, John Bolt, John Koger, David Rogers, Joseph Koger, George Penn, Henry Tuggle, Moses Walden, Amos Rowark, David Harber. Verdict for Pltf.
-Koger vs Shelton, jury sworn: Martin Amoss, Humphrey Smith, John Bolt, David Rogers, Moses Walden, William McCrary, Edward Tatum, Nathan Hall, David Harbour, Isham Cradock, Martin Sims, Henry Tuggle. Verdict retd for Pltf, new tryall granted Defd.
-On the motion ofWilliam Amoss, an injunction is granted him to stay the proceedings of a Judgment obtained against him by Stephen Lyon assignee of John Henderson until same can be heard in Equity. His security for bond, Martin Amos.
-Power of attorney from John Henderson to James Taylor

PAGE 23

-Koger vs Shelton, jury sworn: Benjamin Kimzey, William McPeak, Hamburston Lyon, William Amoss, Jacob Lawson, Samuel Kennon, Joseph King, Jonah Bryant, Amoss Rowark, Joseph Reynolds, George Stults, John Wallace. Verdict for Defd.
-Adams assignee vs Jarett
-Benjamin Garrett appointed to recognizance taken before James Lyon, Justice, with William Carter his security. Indebeted to the Commonwealth, to be of good behavior to the citizens and especially towards George Rogers.
-George Penn, Hamon Critz, Edward Tatum, Munford Smith, John Ellison, Charles Thomas and David Harber are recommended as fit persons to serve as Justice of the Peace.
Court Wednesday 13 March 1793 present: Abram Penn, Charles Foster, Samuel Clark, Francis Turner, William Carter.
-On the motion of Henry Koger by his attorney, a new tryall granted him against Samuel Shelton.
-Commonwealth vs Smith
-Lyne vs King
-King vs Cradock, Pltf to take depo of Dunn Salyiars, Ambrose Mullins and David Wilkinson.

Page 23 contd

-Jones	vs Wright
-Gees	vs Salsberry
-Lyne	vs King
-Maberry	vs Tuggle
-King	vs Cradock
-Anglin	vs Newman, referred to John Dillard and William Banks.

PAGE 24

-Benson ?	vs Cooper
-Chandler	vs Going
-Hanby	vs Lyon
-Charles	vs Hickenbottom
-Turner	vs Noe
-Thompkins	vs Lewis

-The order recommending several Justices of the Peace yesterday is considered by the Court not to be expedient, therefore, the same is rescinded.
-Samuel Staples and Thomas Mitchell are appointed to let to the lowest bidder repairs to the Jail after advertising same for 2 weeks, money to be paid out of depositum.
Court Monday 8 April 1793 present: Abram Penn, James Lyon, Francis Turner, William Carter

-Deed- Peter Vess and John Dunkin to John Spencer
-Deed- Andrew Woolverton to John Medley
-Deed- Richard Welch to Peter Duncan, Liddy Welch, wife of Richard Welch, relinquishes her right of dower
-Deed- John Watson to William Heath
-Deed- John Watson to John W. Watson
-Deed- Elisabeth Sizms to Mesheck Barrett
-Power of attorney from William Weatherspoon to S. Daniel

PAGE 25

-Deed- Samuel Allen to James Poteet Jr
-Deed- James Herron to Uriah Leftwich
-Deed- James Bedford Jr to Uriah Leftwich
-Deed- William Barton and wife Seppy to Thomas Barton
-Deed- Andrew Polson to Richard Polson
-Seppy Barton wife of William Barton, relinquishes her right of dower to the deed of 100 acres conveyed to Sharp Barton.
-Deed- Hamon Critz Jr to Richard Hopkins
-Deed- John Marr to Bethany Letcher
-Deed- John Marr to Joseph Francis
-Deed- John Marr to John Douglas
-Deed- William Greer to Joseph Pratt
-Deed- Andrew Woolverton to Samuel Clark Jr
-Deed- John Hammons Jr to Joseph Apling, Mary Hammons wife of John Hammons relinquishes her right of dower.

Court Tuesday 9 April 1793 present: Abraham Penn, James Armstrong, Francis Turner, Charles Foster
-Barrett vs Lawson, Pltf to take depo of John Fields and William Mankins
-Deed- David Davis to Thomas Ayrs
-Garrott vs Lawson and wife, Defd to take depo of Jeremiah Rick and Andrew Polson (of NC) and Richard Terry.
-James Dickenson appointed surveyor of the road from William Griffins to Wards Gap Road, list filed.

PAGE 26

-Read	vs Going	-Lackey vs Tuggle
-Frazor	vs Berry	-Copley vs Vess
-Hairston	vs Tittle	-Saunders vs Tuggle
-Keaton	vs Turner	-Holt vs Small
-Holt	vs Kimzey	-Pigg vs Sharp

Page 26 contd

-Kimzey vs Morris
-Smith vs Cooper, George Tittle a garnishee saith he has a horse of the defendants in his possession.
-Lee & Adkins vs Bowman
-On the motion of Mathew Small to stay proceedings against brought by John Bolt till he can be heard in Equity
-Long vs Turner
-Job Ross appointed surveyor of the road in place of Jacob Johnson from Carolina to the top of the mountain at Wards Gap.
-A report of a view of a road from Abners Ridge into the same road again a short distance from William Hancocks.
-George Dodson Sr, John Pulliam, John Randalls and William Sharp to view a way for a road out of the road called Bull Mountain Rd above Newmans to John Cammerons.
-Tatum vs William Willis, Joel Willis a granishee being sworn saith he owes the defendant Ł13.8.
-A receipt from Daniel Carlin to John Hammons produced in Court.
-Nathan Littrell is appointed surveyor of the road in place of John Sharp from Patrick Courthouse into the road near Shadrick Barretts.
-Lot Litrell appointed surveyor of the road in place of Jacob Adams Jr from Adams to the South Mayo.
-Deed- Holden McGee to Stephen Lyon
-Puckett vs Lyon, Harvey Fitzgerald, David Rogers, Abraham Frazor and James Lyon Jr Spl Bl.

PAGE 27

-On a motion of Stephen Lyon by his attorney, to squash an escape issued in favor of Joseph Bolding against said Lyon and in consideration whereof this Court are of the opinion that the said escape warrant was null and void as there is a judgment against said Defendant prior to the execution of the escape.
-Abraham Penn and Charles Foster descent from the above opinion.
-On the motion of Jeremiah Burnett Sr leave is granted him to keep an Ordinary at this Courthouse with Samuel Staples his security.
-The Court sets the following rates: Diets, for a Dinner if hot 1/6; Stableage of 1 horse 24 hours 9d; Fodder if bundled 1d, Cyder,gallon 2/6.
-Abraham Penn, Archelaus Hughes, James Lyon or any 2, appointed to let the building of a Courthouse for the use of this County. To be 36 ft x 24 ft, 2 jury rooms at one end 12 ft square and brick or stone chimney with a fireplace to each jury room. The house to be 12 ft pitch with Barr and seats. Walls to be timber, brick or stone. The roof sheated and shingled. If framed, good sound timer feather-edge planked; 4 panel door with locks and hinges. Two 18-light windows, one on each side of the Justices room. 2 sheriffs boxes with a small window at each box. Two 12-light windows at the end, also 1 18-light window, one for each jury room. The sides and ends nicely sealed. The joists to be lathed and plastered. All of which is to be done in a good workmanlike manner, to be completed on or before 1 October 1794. The undertaker will be paid Ł50. within two months from letting the Courthouse and Ł 50. within six months afterward and the balance when finished and received by the Court.

PAGE 28

Court Tuesday 9 April 1793 present: Abraham Penn, James Lyon, Samuel Clark, William Carter. For the examination of John Poteet on suspicion of a felony. Said Poteet, John, failing to appear, the State Attorney is to promote said Poteet and secure.
-Court 13 May 1793 present: James Lyon, James Armstrong, Samuel Clark and William Banks.
-Peter Stolts is exempt from the payment of county and parish levies for the future.
-A negro man slave Nimrod Dunmore, is the property of James Taylor.
-Deed- Eliphaz Shelton to John Yeats alias Smith, Nancy Shelton wife of Eliphaz Shelton relinquishes her right of dower to the 72 acres.

Page 28 contd

-Jury: Isaac Adams foreman, William Deal, James Thompson, John Adams, Henry McGuffey, James Hale, Harris Carter, William Sharp, Tandy Senter, Miller Easley, William James Mayo, Mathew Small, William Easley, Jacob Adams Sr, Josiah Farris, Robert Hall, all sworn as Grand Jury.
-Mabray Jr vs Tuggle
-Hairston vs McGeehe
-Hill vs McGeehe
-Hughes vs McGeehe
-Lyon vs Sams
-Deed- Benjamin Garrett to George Garrett
-Deed- William Allen to Peter Stolts
-Kimzey vs Morris, referred to James Denny, Richard Pilson, William Isom and Joseph Reynolds
-Kimzey vs Thomas and Job Gees, referred to above

PAGE 29

-The Grand Jury made several presentments.
-Leave is granted Gabriel Penn to keep an Ordinary at this Court, bond with George Penn his security.
-Forbis vs Hammonds Jr, Samuel Kennon Spl Bl
-Laurance vs Dickerson
-Pigg vs Sharp
-Present at Court: Francis Turner, Jonathan Hanby, William Carter
-Deed- Joseph Johnson to Stephen Jones
-Deed- Samuel Allen to James Poteet Jr
-Deed- William Green to Joseph Pratt
-George Penn, Hamon Critz Jr, Edward Tatum, Brett Stovall, Munford Smith, Charles Thomas, John Ellison, John Braden Jr are received as Justices of the Peace.
-Deweese vs Tittle
-Deed- John Rea to Aaron------
-Pierce Giun is exempt from the payment of county and parish levies for the future.
-Frazor vs Berry
-Deed- Andrew Herren to John Simmon
-Nathaniel Harris is allowed 1 day as witness for Berry vs Frazor
-Sanders vs Tuggle
-Adams vs Going
-Coday vs Boyd
-Smith vs Johnson
-Boyd vs Kelly
-Hall vs Kimzey
-Morris vs Kimzey
-Rickman vs Reynolds
-Kelly vs James Boyd
-Detheridge vs Hickman

PAGE 30

-Power of attorney of Nicholas Baker given to James Armstrong.
-John Hammonds ear mark, a smooth cross and under keel in each ear and also brnad: I.H.
-Nathan Hall is order to appear at the next Court to answer for not reporting his taxable property.
-Brown vs Griffin
-The difference between J. Bolt and Mathew Small is referred to Charles Thomas, David Harbour, Charles Ferrell and Jesse Corn.
Court Tuesday 14 May 1793 present: James Lyon, Stephen Lyon, William Carter, Francis Turner, Jonathan Hanby.
-Barrett vs Lawson, Jacob Lawson Spl Bl
-Senter vs Hammonds Jr
-Smith vs Burnett
-Smith vs Wingo
-Bryant vs Willis
-Smith vs Lewis
-Hairston vs Tittle
-On a motion of Robert Wilson & Company by his attorney, judgment to them on a delivery bond against Hamon France as security for Benjamin Philpott and costs.
-On a motion of John Copley by his attorney, judgment granted him on a delivery bond against Azariah Shelton and Hamon Critz.
-John Hooker and John Botetourt on a delivery bond with costs.
-John Henderson gives power of attorney to James Taylor.

Page 30 contd
-Deed- Abraham E. Rowden to Isham Cradock

PAGE 31

-Turner vs Henderson and others
- On the motion of Jacob Adams Jr judgment is granted against Joseph Street on a delivery bond with cost.
-On a motion of John Henderson by E. Henry his attorney, for an injunction to stay a judgment against him by Martin Amoss until it can be hear in Equity. Security Charles Thomas
-Koger vs Shelton (2)
-Lyne vs King
-Gees vs Salsbury
-Charles vs Gilliland and Hickinbottom
-King vs Cradock
-Innes vs Wright
-James Baker is alld 1 day attendance as a witness Lyne vs King and 25 miles
-On a motion of John Wright vs James Innes, defendant to take the depo of Christian Hughes
-Robert White alld 2 days witness for James Innes vs John Wright
-Dunn Solyears 3 days wintess James King vs Cradock
-Brown vs Cooper
-Hanby vs Lyon
-Amos vs Henderson
-Thompkins vs Lewis
-Edward Tatum 1 day witness H. Lyon vs Hanby
-William Lyon 2 days for same
-Salsberry vs Geels
-Mankin vs Senter, John Mankin security for cost
-Jury sworn: James Taylor, Nathan Hall, Isham, Cradock, Edward Lewis, William McAlexander, Samuel Kennon, David Rogers, Nathaniel Smith, William Isam, Charles Thomas, William Allen, John Henderson.
-James Bailey 1 day witness Tandy Senter vs Jesse Mankin
-Miller Easley same
-Eliphaz Shelton, for the Pltf same

PAGE 32

-Samuel Staples against Eliphaz Shelton as guardian for Esop Shelton, Abigail Shelton, Liberty Shelton and Mary Shelton. Abram Penn attormey for Ralph Shelton Jr, Palatiah Shelton, Jeremiah Shelton, William McGehee and Julius Robertson also Dudley Rutherford, William Arnold, William Jones, Roger Shelton, Azariah Shelton, Ezekieh Shelton, James Shelton, heirs of Ralph Shelton dec'd, defendants.
-The defendants Dudley Rutherford, William Jones and William Arnold not having given security and not inhabitants of this county. The defendants are to appear the 2nd Monday of August and answer complaint. Copy to be inserted in the Virginia Gazette for two months.
-Lyon vs Lane, judgment, Edward Tatum garnishee
-Pennington vs Polson
-Kennon vs Gibson
-Lawson and wife vs Garrott
-Rich vs Hambleton
-Mary Moses allowed 2 days witness B. Lawson vs Garrett
-Lisa Lawson the same
-John Rick 2 days witness Benjamin Garrett vs David Lawson and wife
-Moses Reynolds allowed 15/ for keeping William Rickmans cattle and removing the same.
-Koger vs Copley
-Mankin vs Senter, Pltf take depo of Tabithia Charles
-Rickman vs Pulliman, referred to Alexander Hunter & Charles Croucher.
-Perego vs Soloman
-Lawson vs Garrett

PAGE 33

At a Court held for Patrick County Monday 10 June 1793 present: A. Hughes, Charles Foster, William Carter, Jonathan Hanby, James Lyon, Samuel Clark, Abraham Penn.
-Deed- Mathew Small to John Breden, Jane Small wife of Mathew Small, relinquishes her right of dower
-Deed- Archelaus Hughes to Brett Stovall - 2 deeds
-Deed- Daniel Howell to Francis Turner
-Deed- Arthur Parr to David Keaton
-Deed- Micajah Frazor to George Hairston
-Thorp vs Wingo
-Lackey vs Tuggle
-A report of a view of a road from Samuel Corns path out of the Hollow Road to Hughes Road returned
-also from where the road leaves Bull Mtn Rd above Newmans to John Camerons, returned
-Also from Corns Rd near Harbers Shop to Samuel Laws returned
-Stephen vs Tatum
-Perigo vs Salmon
-Joseph Taylor is appointed surveyor of the road in place of John Wright from the cross roads at the little meadows to the Henry line.
-George Corn is appointed surveyor of the road in place of Peter Corn from the South Mayo to Spoon Creek.
-Joseph Stovall is recommended as a fit person to serve as a Commissioner for the County.
-Commonwealth vs Holt for concealing his taxable property;for reasons appearing to the satisfaction of the Court, case dismissed.

PAGE 34

June Court 1793
-Hairston vs Tittle
-Lawson vs Garrott
-Williams Jr vs Tittle
-Hughes & Hairston vs Dickerson
-Wright vs Dunkin
-Willis vs Stephens
-Hall vs Kimzey
-Lyon vs Scott
-Stephens vs Elkins
-Stephens vs Branham
-Shelton vs Fields & Collings
-Lyon vs Small
-John Wilson appointed surveyor of the road in the place of Joseph Francis from Dry Pond to the Widow Easleys.
-William Smiths hands, Woody Burge, Jonathan Hanby, Joseph Going, Thomas Hornsby, Herbert Smith are added to the list of Edward Tatums from the forks of the road above Stephen Lyons to Peters Creek in Hanbys lane.
-Court 8 July 1793 present: A. Hughes, Francis Turner, James Armstrong, Samuel Clark, James Lyon.
-Spurlock vs Poteet
-Deed- Micajah Frazor to George Hairston
-Bolt vs Small
-Gabriel Penn is allowed 26/. for keeping and removing negros, the property of N. Hall.
-Edward Tatum produced a list of taxable property for 1793 and is allowed 67 days for his service.

PAGE 35

-Adam Tittle with Anthony Tittle give bond, on condition of being on good behavior, especially to Patty Richards, 12 months 1 day.
-Lyon vs Small, on an attachment, John Breden Sr a garnishee being sworn saith he owes nothings; dismissed.
-Lawson vs Garrott
-Stephens vs Elkins
-Penn vs Hall & Barnard
-Adkinson vs Scott
-Lyon vs Scott
-Stephens vs Branham
-Cole vs Bowman
-Adkinson vs Thomas Scott
Present: A. Hughes, James Lyon, James Armstrong, Stephen Lyon, William Carter, Francis Turner.
-Daniel Carlin, Samuel Clark and William Carter are recommended as fit persons to serve as Sherif.
-Hamon Critz Jr and John Breden Jr are appointed to inspect the repairs to the Jail and report.

Page 35 contd

-The report is that the work has been done sufficiently.
-Ordered to pay Gabriel Penn 28/. for repairs to the County Jail.
-Hamon Critz Jr is recommended as a fit and proper person to serve as Colonel Commandant for the County
-Lawson vs Garrott, plantiffs security: George Rogers Jr.
-On a motion of William B. Price for an injunction to stay a judgment against him by William Adams, granted with John Poteet his security.
-Penn vs Hall and Barnard
-John Henderson allowed 10 days witness Penn vs Barnard and Ha..

PAGE 36

Court Tuesday 9 July 1793 present: A. Hughes, Abram Penn, Samuel Clark, William Carter, Jonathan Hanby, Stephen Lyon.
-Stephen Lyon is recommended as Major of the 1st Battalion and William Carter Major of the 2nd.
-Jesse Corn recommended as Captain of the 1st Btn; James Turner Lt; George Mabe Ensign.
-John Poteet recommended as Captain; George Lackey Lt; James Poteet Jr as Ensign.
-Jacob Critz as Captain; Brett Stovall as Lt; Peter Corn as Ensign.
-Samuel Crutcher as Capt; William Sharp as Lt; Charles Hebert as Ensign
-Charles Foster as Capt; William Adams Lt; William B. Price,Ensign.
-Henry Smith as Capt of 2nd Btn; James Lyon Lt; John Tatum Ensign.
-Munford Smith as Capt; Robert Hudspeth as Lt; William Moore as Ensign.
-William Griffin as Capt; John Jarett as Lt; Tandy Senter as Ensign.
-John Parr Jr as Capt; Hamon Shelton as Lt; George Rogers Jr Ensign.
-Joseph Stovall recommended as Captain of a Company of Riflemen of the 1st Btn; John Frans Lt; Leander Hughes Ensign.
-Samuel Staples Capt of 2nd Btn; John Hanby Lt; Jesse Tatum Ensign
-Ordered that the citizens of the town of Taylorsville, except Samuel Staples, be added to Eliphaz Sheltons list.

PAGE 37

Court 12 August 1793 present: William Banks, James Armstrong, William Carter, Charles Foster, James Lyon, Francis Turner
-Lyne vs Redman
-Deed- Bartlett Reynolds to Thomas Hambleton
-Deed- Joseph Johnson to Joseph Jackson
-Goerge Penn Jr, Hamon Critz, Edward Tatum, Brett Stovall, Munford Smith, Charles Thomas, John Breden Jr, Joseph Stovall took the oath of Justices of the Peace.
-Administration of the estate of John Lackey dec'd is granted Peter Saunders with George Hairston his security.
-William Gardner, John Koger and David Harbour to appraise same estate.
-David Patterson, Barnard Markham, Young Short and Benjamin ______ to appraise the estate of John Lackey in Chesterfield County.
-Appointed as Grand Jury: James Taylor foreman, Tandy Senter, Obediah Hudson, Henry Smith, James Ferrell, Hamon France, Benjamin Hancock, William Bennett, Richard Pilson, William McAlexander, William Isom, Zepharniah Tenison, Samuel Pusey, William Gilliam, Golder Davidson, Anthony Collings.
-Overseers of the Poor to bind out Mathew Morgan. Also Rachel Mullins, William Mullins, Green Mullins, Washington Mullins, Daniel Mullins, Jemimah Mullins, John Mullins & Alexander Mullins poor orphans of Mathew Mullins deceased.
-Anglin vs Newman

PAGE 38

-On a motion of Joseph Jackson leave is granted him to keep an Ordinary at his house with Munford Smith his security.
-Redman vs Pulliam, Pltf to take depo of Richard Collins
-Isham vs Poteet
-Deed- Augustine Brown to Samuel Hooker, Mary Brown wife of Augustine Brown relingquishes her right of dower.

Page 38 contd

-Koger vs Redman, John France Spl Bl
-Lyon vs Scott
-Kimzey vs Gee
-Hamon Critz gentleman, produced a commission appointing him Lieutenant Colonel Commandant of the 18th Regt of Militia.
-Stephen vs Branham, Pltf to take depo of Michael Warden
-Deed- William Halbert to William Smith, Jr
-Commonwealth vs Johnson
-same vs Dunkin
-Same vs Rose
-same vs Hall
-same vs Hawks
-same vs Kimzey
-Saunders vs Harris
-Kennon vs Gibson
-Stephen vs Branham, defd take depo of Barna Barnham.

PAGE 39

Court Tuesday 13 August 1793 present: A. Hughes, George Penn, Brett Stovall, Francis Turner, James Armstrong

-Koger vs Shelton
-Gee vs Salsberry
-Innes vs Wright
-Puckett vs Lyon
-Amos vs Henderson
-Salsberry vs Gee
-Pennington vs Polson
-Lyne vs King
-King vs Cradock
-Brown vs Cooper
-Hanby vs Lyon
-Thompkins vs Lewis
-Mankin vs Senter
-Kennon vs Gibson
-Lawson and wife vs Garrott for slander
-Innes, an infant, vs Wright
-Grand Jury: Woody Burge, David Rogers, William Adams, John Hancock, Moses Walden, John Bolt, Nathan Hall, Joseph Koger, John Koger, Thomas Hall, Edward Lewis, Jacob Adams Sr .
-Robert White allowed 3 days witness Innis vs Wright
-Saunders vs Harrison, William McPeak Spl Bl
-Deed- Benjamin Hawkins to Pleasant Sowell
-Lyne vs King, jury sworn: William Amoss, John Hall, William B.Price, Amos Rowark, Henry Smith, David Rowark, William McPeak, Humphrey Smith, James Baker, Dunn Solyears, Charles Dodson, John Hammonds Jr.
-King vs Cradock, jury sworn: Woody Burge, David Rogers, John Hancock, Moses Walden, John Bolt, Joseph Koger, Thomas Hall, John Koger, Jacob Adams Jr, Edward Lewis, Jeremiah Burnett, David Morgan, verdict returned for defendant.
-John Hooker 2 days witness Joseph King vs Isham Cradock.

PAGE 40

-Mankin vs Senter, jury sworn: Thomas Hudson, Jesse Tatum, Obediah Hudson, William McPeak, Harvey Fitzgerald, Amos Rowark, William Hickenbottom, Dunn Solyears, Charles Dodson, Thomas Willis, James Kennon, John Wright..verdict for Pltf..one penny damages.
-James Lyon, gentleman burser to collect money arising from the lots sold in the Town of Taylorsville.
-Deed- William Adams to William Price
-James Baker allowed 1 day 25 miles witness I. Cradock vs Joseph King
-Moses Walden 3 days for same
-William Adams Sr 5 days for same
-Miller Easley 1 day witness Senter vs Mankins
-James Bailey 1 day for same
-Eliphaz Shelton 1 day witness Jesse Mankin vs T. Senter
-Archelaus Shelton 1 day for same
-Dunn Solyears 4 days for J. King vs I. Cradock
-Lawson and wife vs Garrott, jury sworn, non-suit granted defendant.
-same for same, for slander; jury sworn: William Adams, John Hammons, Moses Walden, Charles Dodson, Isham Cradock, William B.Price, Abraham Eads, Nathaniel Smith, Joseph Keaton, George Fulcher, Samuel Carter,

Page 40 contd

William Adams Jr, verdict returned for defendant.

PAGE 41

Court Wednesday 14 August 1793 present: Abraham Penn, James Lyon, Francis Turner, Joseph Stovall, Stephen Lyon.
-Eliphaz Shelton appointed guardian for Esop Shelton, Abigail Shelton, Mary Shelton, Liberty Shelton infants and heirs of Ralph Shelton dec'd to answer a Bill in Chancery exhibited against James Shelton.
-Wilson & Co vs Lyon
-Pennington vs Polson, deposition of Zackeriah Stanley be taken
-Rich vs Hambleton, referred to John Nunn and John Bolt
-Burnett vs Mayo, Burnett take depo of Sally Burnett
-Lawson vs Garrott
-Adams vs Mankin & Keaton, jury sworn: William Amos, William James Mayo, Samuel Dalton, Humphrey Smith, James Shelton, ______ Hickenbottom, David Morgan, William Burnett, John Bolt, Joseph Gowin, Jeremiah Burnett, John Hammond Jr, verdict for Pltf.
-Joel Mans?? allowed 4 days witness Lawson vs Garrett
-Elisha Lawson 2 days for same
-Henry Boling 1 day for same
-Andrew Polson 1 day for same
-Nancy Polson same
and Betsy the same

PAGE 42

-Moses vs Mitchell referred to James Lyon, William Carter, Stephen Lyon.
-Elisha Lawson vs Mitchell
-Forbas vs Hammons, defendant take depo of Ben Benson
-Garrott vs Lawson, dismissed

Court 9 September 1793 present: Archelaus Hughes, John Braden, William Carter, Stephen Lyon, Hamon Critz, Charles Thomas.
-Deed- John Matthews to Archelaus Hughes
-Deed- William Mills to Richard Mills
-Deed- Robert Woods to Michael Kelly
-Deed- Michael Kelley to Isham Puckett
-On the motion of Elisabeth Bennett leave is granted her to build a water grist mill on the Middle Fork of the Little Dan, she being the owner on both sides.
-On a motion of James Shelton by his attorney, a general commission is awarded him and advertise parties to take depositions.
-Levy Pedigo appointed surveyor of the road in place of Charles Thomas from Shooting Crk. to Joint Crack Creek.
-Thomas R. Hall is appointed Constable
-Rickman vs Pulliam, award to Pltf.
-Webb vs Burge, dismd

PAGE 43

-Stephen vs Branham
-Adkinson vs Thomas Scott
-Smith vs Kimzey
-Stephen vs Elkins
-Adkinson vs W. Scott
-Tatum vs William Mankin
-Isaac Adams presented credentials of his Ordination of the Baptist Church and entered into Bond.
-Baker vs Griffin
-Smith vs Barnard
-Gibson vs Polson
-Staples vs Shelton
-Penn vs Shelton
-Laurence vs Boyd
-On a motion of John Koger to build a water grist mill on the north fork of Gobling Town Creek, he owns on one side.
-Richard Terry allowed 2 days witness Benjamin Garett against David Lawson and Sarah Lawson his wife.
-Moses Rea same
-Laurance vs Boyd, Sheriff has leave to amend his return of the petition.
-John Koger allowed 3 days witness Joseph King vs Henry Lyne.

Page 43 contd

-Deed- Lucy Barnard to Humphrey Smith
-Power of attorney from William Banks to Elisha Adams
-Joseph Keaton appointed surveyor of the road in place of Peter France from Spoon Creek above Hamon Critz into the Hollow Roa dat Magruders Cabin.

PAGE 44

Court Monday 14 October 1793 present: A. Hughes, William Banks, Samuel Clark, Francis Turner

-Deed- Bartlett Foley to John Kindley
-Deed- Archelaus Hughes to James and William Sublett
-Deed- John Lewiston to Hugh Innes
-Deed- William Taylor to George Hairston
-Deed- Micajah Frazer to George Hairston
-Deed- William Isam to Isham Burnett
-Deed- William Woody to Hugh Innes
-An inventory of the estate of John Lackey, dec'd returned.
-Marr vs Mitchell
-Lawson vs Mitchell
-Deed- John Matthews to Archelaus Hughes
-Deed- Wood to Hugh Innes further proved
-Thomas Bristoe is appointed Constable in room of Alexander Frazor.
-Deed- Azariah Shelton to Lott Littrell, Sarah Shelton, wife of Azariah, relinquishes her right of dower
-Ann Tittle vs Patty Richards, dismissed
-Deed- James Buford to Eliphaz Shelton
-A power of attorney from Hannah Mayo to Jesse Corn
-Stephens vs Branham
-Robert Hall, with security Jacob Lawson and Golder Davison, appeared in Court to post Bond in the case of Nathan Going.

PAGE 45

Court Wednesday 30 October 1793 present: Jonathan Hanby, A. Hughes, William Carter, Edward Tatum.
-On the examination of George Joyce on suspicion of feloniously stealing a negro man Jack the property of Stephen Lyon. The prisoner was led to the Barr by William Mitchell Sheriff and found not guilty.

PAGE 46

Court Monday 4 November 1793 present: Charles Thomas, James Armstrong, James Lyon, John Braden, Edward Tatu, Abraham Penn
-Deed- James Charles to Michael Ahart
-Jury sworn: George Rogers Sr foreman, Jacob Adams Sr, James Ferrell, John Sharp, William Sharp, Henry Smith, Miller Easley, George Penn, William Witt, Thomas Dillard, Golder Davison, Sharp Barton, William Burnett, William McAlexander, William Isom, James Pigg, William James Mayo.
-Clough Shelton & Co vs Henry Tuggle, John Tuggle
-Coleman vs Frans
-Daniel Carlin, gentleman, produced a commission appointing him Sherif, took the usual oaths with James Armstrong, James Lyon, Munford Smith and Edward Tatum as his security.
-Thomas Mitchell admitted as Deputy Sherif
-Hughes vs L. Manning, Thomas Mitchell Spl Bl
-McGhee vs Charles, Daniel Carlin Spl Bl, defendant to take the depo of William Burns and William McCraw.
-Williamson & Garland vs Taylor, Hamon France Spl Bl
-Commonwealth vs B. Smith
-McCrary vs Griffin, pltf to take depo of Claborn Lawrence; Munford Smith, Miller Easley security for Pltf.

PAGE 47

Court Monday 11 November 1793 present: James Lyon, William Carter, Francis Turner, Brett Stovall, James Armstrong, John Braden Jr, Munford Smith, Stephen Lyon, Charles Thomas.
-On the examination of a negro man slave John, the property of Samuel Staples and Gabriel Penn, on suspicion of stealing 1 broadcloth coat, 1 pr breeches, 1 shirt and 1 pr shoes valued at L4.3. Taken from the house of Jacob Lawson. Said John, in custody of Daniel Carlin, plead not guilty. The Court judged him guilty and he shall receive 39 lashes on his bare back and be branded with an R on his jaw.

Court-present: William Carter, Edward Tatum, Charles Thomas and Munford Smith.
-Hairston vs Redman, John Ellis Spl Bl also William Garner.
-Ordered that the Sherif pay Charles Vest 50 pounds.
-Pulliam vs Cranch, Moses Joseph Reynolds Spl Bl.

PAGE 48

Court Tuesday 12 November 1793 present: Abraham Penn, Charles Thomas, Francis Turner, John Braden Jr.
-Commonwealth vs Francis
-same vs Frazor
-Lyne vs King
-Koger vs Redman
-Moore vs Going
-Isom vs Poteet, jury sworn: John Ferrell, Humphrey Smith, Valentine Mayo, James McBride, John Burnett, Isham Cradock, John Koger, Henry Hanes, David Rogers, George Brooks, Henry Harrison Deen.
-Koger vs Shelton
-Cradock vs King
-Allen vs Johnson
-Smith vs Frazer
-Inquisition on the body of Nathan Going returned.
-Deed- Thomas Mitchell to James Poteet Jr
-Ordered that William Banks take possession of the estate of his mother Ann Banks, devised to her by her husband,deceased, that he support and maintain her of the profits during her lifetime. Gabriel Penn and Samuel Croucher appointed trustees for Ann Banks.

PAGE 49

Court Tuesday 12 November 1793 present: Abram Penn, James Lyon, Stephen Lyon, William Banks, Francis Turner, Edward Tatum.
-Robert Hall to be examined on suspicion of murdering Nathan Going. Led to the Bar by Daniel Carlin, Sherif, plead not guilty, Court finds him not guilty.
Court Wednesday 13 November 1793 present: William Banks, Samuel Clark, James Braden Jr, Francis Turner.
-Puckett vs Lyon
-Brown vs Cooper
-Salsberry vs Gee
-Saunders vs Harris, jury sworn: Jacob McCraw, Gabriel Penn, Samuel Clark, Samuel Kennon, William Burnett, David Rogers,William McCrary, John Burnett, John Cammerson, Jeremiah Burnett, John Ferrell, Daid Witt..verdict for Pltf.
-Pennington vs Polson
-John Burnett 2 days witness Gee vs Salsberry
-Forbus vs Hammonds Jr, jury sworn: Gabriel Penn, Samuel Clark Jr, William Burnett, David Rogers, William McCrary, John Burnett, Jeremiah Burnett, John Cammeron, David Witt, John Ferrell, Jesse Tatum, John Koger.

PAGE 50

-Smith vs Chandler
-Dockery vs Frans
-Burnett vs Mayo's executors; jury sworn: John Hammons, Isham Burnett,

Page 50 contd

James Shelton, William Rogers, Moses Rogers, Daniel Rowark, Joseph Reynolds, Jacob McCraw, David Morgan, Samuel Kennon, Beveridge Hughes, Joseph Reynolds, Martin Amoss..verdict for Pltf.
-Blackley vs Koger and others
-William Burnett allowed 5 days witness Obediah Burnett vs Mayo exors.
-David Morgan allowed 3 days witness Obediah Burnett vs Mayo exors.
-Sarah Burnett 5 days for same
-Kennon vs Gibson, jury sworn: William Burnett, Moses Reynolds, George Maberry, John Ferrell, Isham Burnett, Martin Amoss, James Shelton..verdict for Pltf with interest from Sept 1790.

-Lyon	vs Scott	-Baker vs Griffin
-Staples	vs Shelton	-Staples vs Parr
-McGee	vs Charles	-Barker vs Maberry
-Maberry	vs Barker	-W. Amoss vs Lyon
-Allen	vs Pipes	-El Barker vs Martin

-Davison vs Lawson referred to James Lyon, William Carter, Edward Tatum.

PAGE 51

-On the motion of Samuel Staples and John Ferrell on______vs Joseph King for rent due...case of John Finch dismissed.
-Ordered that the Sherif in the....sale....Cradock vs King 1/. per day for keeping a horse by virtue of the attorney.
-Kimzey vs Gee
The County for the year 1793

Clerks annual salary	25.
Sheriffs annual salary	25.
Deputy States Attorney salary	25.
	75.

Court Monday 9 December 1793 present: Hamon Critz Jr, Brett Stovall, Charles Thomas, John Braden Jr, Samuel Clark
-Deed- William Mills to Richard Mills
-Archelaus Hughes Jr qualified as Deputy Sherif for Daniel Carlin.
-Deed- John Breden Sr to John Breden Jr
-Deed- John Litrell to William Spencer
-Deed- William Isham to Isham Burnett
-Deed- William Isham to Luke Foley
-Deed- William Woody to Hughes Innes Jr
-Shelton vs Shelton

PAGE 52

-Administration of the estate of Bartlett Foley deceased, is granted Cornelius Deweese with David Morgan his security.
-Humphrey Smith, John Koger, John Ferrell, Moses Walden are to appraise said estate.
-Stephen vs Branham
-George Corn 6 days witness Sol. Stephens vs William Branham
-Sarah Stephen 5 days for same
-Kiziah Stephens 1 day for same
-Stephens vs Elkins
-Reynolds vs Hooker
Court Tuesday 10 December 1793 present: Abram Penn, James Lyon, Samuel Clark, Stephen Lyon and Charles Thomas.
-Administration of the estate of Nathan Going, deceased is granted Shadrick Going. Thomas Ward and Joshua Adams his security.
-Obediah Hudson, John Rea, John Nunn and James Taylor to appraise the estate.
-Deed- Azariah Shelton to Robert Rowan, Sarah Shelton wife of Azariah Shelton, relinquishes right of dower to the 181 acs.
-Overseers of the Poor bind out Liddy Litten, Prisey Litten, Jinney Litten and Barton Litten after the 1st of March next provided they are found burdensome to the Parish.
-John Litten appeared in Court and the prosecutor Leann Spray not appearing therefore he is discharged out of custody.
-Thomas Ward is exempt from further payment of county and parish levies.

PAGE 53

-Williamson & Garland vs Taylor, Peter Leak and Thomas Ward Spl Bl.

County Levy for 1793 brt frwd	75.
to negro Cas 1 old wolf head	2.8
Gabriel Penn as Jailor	8.13
George Brooks, guarding 12 days negro John	6.25
Williamson Deal Sr same for 3 days	1.55
Thomas Mitchell called Court over John Poteet	4.18
same on George Joyce	4.18
same on negro John	4.18
same on Robert Hall	4.18
William Runnolds - 7 young wolf heads	7.30
Clerk for called Court for James Poteet	4.18
same for George Joyce	4.18
same for negro John	4.18
same for Robert Hall	4.18
	$ 135.30

-Goings vs Eckolls, Edward Lewis saith Defendant owes him 84 pounds in trade, said Lewis to obtain a title to a certain tract of land, also Plantiff makes the Defendant a title to a tract of land in North Carolina agreeable to a former contract.

-Bolling vs Bolling
-Smith vs Kimzey
-Gibson vs Hooker
-Tatum vs Mankin
-Baker vs Griffin
-Lyon vs Maness ?

PAGE 54

-Lyne vs Sowell
-Laurance vs Boyd
-Adkinson vs Boyd
-Moore assignee vs Shelton
-same vs Dodson
-Lyne vs Dove
-Gardner vs Barker
-Gibson vs Polson
-Corn vs Barker
-Moore assignee vs Rowark
-same vs Hammon Jr
-same vs Dove
-Hill vs Barker

-William Becknett is appointed surveyor of the road from the County line to the top of the mountain at Flowers Gap in room of Stephen Senter.

-John Gossett continued as surveyor of the road from the Henry line to Tanzeys Path that crosses the Bull Mountain Road.

-Moses Godard appointed surveyor of the road from the top of the Bull Mountain to Tanzeys Path where it crosses the Bull Mountain Road in place of John Gossett.

-Ordered that the Judge of this Court do assign the several bonds for lots sold in the Town of Taylorsville to James Lyon, Burser for the purpose of bringing suits.

PAGE 55

Court Monday 13 January 1794 present: William Carter, James Lyon, Abraham Penn and Edward Tatum.

The Court Day for this County being altered by an act of the last session of Assembly. Therefore, ordered the Court be adjourned until the last Thursday in February next.

Court Monday 10 February 1794 for the purpose of examining a negro man slave known by the name of John, the property of Gabriel Penn and Samuel Staples on suspicion of felony. Present: Samuel Clark, William Banks, Brett Stovall, John Breden Jr, Charles Foster, Edward Tatum, Hamon Critz and William Carter.

The said John ălias "Sunk" was led to the Bar by Sheriff Daniel Carlin and plead not guilty. The Court examined diver witness on behalf of the Commonwealth and find the prisoner Guilty. To receive 20 lashes on his bare back and be discharged out of custody.

PAGE 56

Quarterly session Thursday 27 February 1794 present: Brett Stovall, Charles Foster, William Banks, Geore Penn.

Page 56 contd

-Adam Tittle 4 days witness Anthony Tittle vs George Hairston
-John M. Bowls 1 day 20 miles for same
-John Hughes is recommended a deputy surveyor under Brett Stovall, to be examined by Humphrey Smith touching his qualifications.
-Elijah Banks came into Court and qualified as Deputy Sheriff under Daniel Carlin
-John Breden Sr foreman, John Peter Corn, Thomas Hollandsworth, William Gilliam, William McAlexander, William Isam, George Penn Sr, David Harbour, William Burnett, John Jones, Henry McGuffey, Samuel Kennon, Stephen Senter, James Taylor, George Dodson sworn as Grand Jury.
-On a motion of Samuel Duvall, gentleman, who gave sufficient assurance to the Court of his being legally licensed to practice Law.
-Bolling vs Bolling
-Inventory of the estate of Bartlett Foley dec'd returned.
-Administration of the estate of Humberston Lyon dec'd is granted William Smith with his securities: James Lyon, A. Hughes, Samuel Clark, John Parr; John Fletcher, David Roger to appraise said estate.
-John Hughes admitted as Deputy Surveyor under Brett Stovall
-Commonwealth vs Francis
-same vs Bunch
-same vs Frazor
-same vs Poteet Sr
-same vs Kimzey

PAGE 57

-Lawson vs Brooks

County Levy for year 1793 brt fwd	$ 135.30
Peter Frans 1 old wolf head	2.8
Josiah Farris same	2.8
Charles Foster 5 young wolf heads	5.2
Richard Stone 1 old wolf head	2.8
to Late Surveyor for the County, proportion for running the dividing line between Patrick and Henry Counties, 12 miles	5.55
Sheriff, for called Court about John	4.18
Clerk for same	4.18
Clerk for inquisition on body of Francis Barrett	1.92
same for Nathan Going	1.92
Clerk for 1 pr handcuffs	.80
Clerk for ---	.18
Humphrey Smith for service rendered	2.25
	$ 169.80

-Commonwealth vs John Poteet
-Adams vs Adams, Samuel Packwood a garnishee being served saith he owes the Defendant nothing..dismissed.
-Ordered the Sheriff to pay Edward Lewis, an invalid pensioner, fifteen pounds out of the collection for 1792.
COURT Friday 28 February 1794 present: Abram Penn, William Banks, George Penn, James Breden Jr, Charles Foster, Samuel Clark.
-Hampton vs John & Boyd
-Puckett vs Ross
-Rakes vs Lewis
-Sumpter vs Reaves
-Joyce vs Lyon
-Kelly vs Ross
-Boyd vs Hampton
-Job Ross Appointed Contable in place of James Charles

PAGE 58

-Hughes vs Samuel Manning jury sworn: Joseph R. Johnson, Job Ross, Edward Lewis, Gabriel Penn, Elihu ----, Stephen Senter, John Braden, James Morrison, Philip Pipes, John Jones, Frederick Fitzgerald, Robert Taylor..verdict for Pltf.
-same vs same
-Koger vs Shelton
-McGee vs Charles
-Robert Hudspeth appointed Overseer of the Poor in place of William

Page 58 contd

Hudspeth.
-Pennington vs Polson, jury sworn: Amos Rowark, James Morrison, Martin Sims, Frederick Fitzgerald, Joseph R. Johnson, John Braden, John Jones, Peter Corn, David Rogers, Jacob Lawson, James Shelton, George Rogers Jr,..verdict returned.
-Salsberry vs Gee, jury sworn: Stephen Senter, William McPeak, William Berry, John Allen, John Hammons, Samuel Clark, John Wallace, Joshua Adams, John Williamson, John Chapman, Job Ross, David Keaton..verdict returned for Defendant.
-Lyon vs Scott
-Staples vs Parr
-Allen vs Pipes
-Wright vs Innes
-Staples vs Shelton
-Maberry Sr vs Barker
-Napier vs Amoss
-John Jones 4 days witness Allen vs Pipes
-Elihu Ayres 1 day for same
-Hairston vs Redman
-McCrary & Wallace vs Griffin
-Williamson & Garland vs Taylor
-Shelton & Co vs Tuggle, jury sworn: Elihu Ayres, William Scott, John Wallace, William Berry, Richard Chandler, Robert Taylor, William Griffin, Martin Amoss, William McPeak, John Williamson, John Pulliam, Eliphaz Shelton, verdict for Pltf.
-McCutchen vs Kimzey
-Crouch vs Pulliam
-Forbes vs Hammond Jr

PAGE 59

-William McPeak 4 days witness for Edward and Thomas Salsberry
-Tatum vs Brown
-Administration of the estate of William Manning,dec'd granted A.Hughes with Samuel Clark and Hamon Critz Jr his security.
-George Carter, Eliphaz Shelton, Harvey Fitzgerald, Robert Hall to appraise said estate.
-Amos vs Stephens, depo of Martin Simms to be taken.
-Gardner vs Barker
COURT Saturday 1 March 1794 present: Abram Penn, James Lyon, Gabriel Penn, Edward Tatum.

Levy for County 1793 brt fwd		169.80
Credit for error		60.26
		109.54
Clerk ofCounty for service to Commonwealth		50.
depositum for county use		300.
Sheriff 6/ for collecting 459.54		27.57
		487.11
to a fraction in favor of County		5.61
By 10% tithes at 45¢ per poll	492.72	492.72

-On a motion of Daniel Carlin by Thomas Mitchell for an objection of the County Jail being insufficient whereupon said Sheriff not considered liable for an escape in that case.
-Gabriel Penn appointed Jailor
-Ordered that several charges in the County levy for the year 1793 for services rendered by the Clerk, Sheriff and Jailor and in criminal prosecutions be null and void, the sum being deducted on the closing of levy.
-Ordered that members now present do fix on a place for the building of the Courthouse.

PAGE 60

COURT Wednesday 9 March 1794 present: Francis Turner, James Stovall, Samuel Clark, Charles Foster, Abram Penn, Edward Tatum, John Breden Jr.
-Court to examine Thomas Garrison on suspicion of Felony. Prisoner was led to the Bar in custody of Daniel Carlin sheriff, plead not guilty. Court find prisoner not guilty.
COURT Thursday 27 March 1794 present: A. Hughes, James Lyon, Samuel Clark, Charles Foster, Gabriel Penn.

Page 60 contd

-Deed- Peter Frans and Hamon Frans and William Banks to John Frans
-Deed- William Cornwell to Jacob Critz
-Deed- William Cornwell to John Miller
-Deed- Augustine Brown to John Willis Jr, Mary Brown wife of Augustine Brown relinquishes her right of dower
-Deed- William Adams to Samuel Packwood
-Deed- Augustine Brown to Samuel Staples
-Hale vs Henry
-Critz vs Cornwell

PAGE 61

-Edmond Staples exempt from payment of County and Parish levies for the future.
-Deed- Isaac Adams to Brett Stovall
-Ordered that James Lyon, Burser, Pay Jacob Adams Jr £4.13.7 out of the money arising from the lots sales in the Town of Taylorsville.
-Power of Attorney of John Henderson to John Koger
-Deed- John Simmon to John D---nesy
-Deed- George Carter to Thomas Hill
-Deed- Augustine Brown to Samuel Hooker
-Inventory of the estate of Humberston Lyon, dec'd, returned
-Hamon Critz Jr, Colonel Commander of this County came into Court and resigned his commission.
-Deed- William Fulcher to Henry Fulcher
-Shelton vs Rowan
-Bowles Abbington appointed surveyor of the road in place of James Slator from the mouth of Penns lane at the banks of the Mayo to the Henry line.
-Esbill ? vs Halbert
-Eliphaz Shelton, Harvey Fitzgerald, Samuel Staples and Gabriel Penn to view a way for a road out of Bull Mtn Rd to Patrick Courthouse.
-William Burnett appointed surveyor of the road from Francis Turners to Mathew Morrows in place of George Maberry Jr.
-James Taylor surveyor of the road from the Mayo at Penns lane to said James Taylors in place of John Pulliam.
-Lawson vs Rowan
-Hairston vs Cornwell, William Gilliam security
-Dickerson vs Adkins

PAGE 62

-George Penn recommended as Colonel Commandant
-Stephen Lyon as Major of the 1st Btn, William Carter of the 2nd.
COURT Wednesday 2 April 1794 present: Jonathan Hanby, Gabriel Penn, Edward Tatum, Samuel Clark, William Carter, James Lyon.
-Court to examine Peter Bowman on suspicion of the murder of Francis Barrett. Prisoner led to the Bar by Sheriff Daniel Carlin, pleads not guilty. Court finds Not Guilty.

PAGE 63

COURT Thursday 24 April 1794 present: Archelaus Hughes, Abraham Penn, James Lyon, Jonathan Hanby.
-Deed- John Wright to George Hairston
-Deed- William Hudspeth to John Creed
-Deed of Gift- William Hudspeth to Carter Hudspeth
-Deed- John Poteet Jr to William Sharp
-Deed- William Sharp to Joel Chitwood
-Deed- Luke Foley to Jacob Saunders
-Deed- George Corn, Peter Corn to Samuel Clark, Dolley and Elisabeth Corn relinquish their right of dower
-Deed- Martin Amoss to Dandridge Slaughter
-Deed- Michael Cloer to George Hairston
-Beed- William Gardner to George Hairston
-Deed- James Poteet Jr to William Sharp
-Deed- Joseph Street to Benjamin Mize
-Deed- Joseph Street to Margaret Bristoe

Page 63 contd

-Susannah Street wife of Samuel Street relinquishes her right of dower.
-Deed- William Branham Sr to John Frans
-Deed- John Kindrick to Moses Hurt
-Deed- David Tittle to Thomas Harbour
-John Lee is exempt from the payment of County and Parish levies for the future
-Joshua Hall the same
-Deed- William Gardner to Samuel Staples
-Daniel Carlin came into Court with Thomas Mitchell, James Armstrong, Jonathan Hanby and William Carter as his security for a Bond for the collection of Tax for 1793.

PAGE 64

COURT Friday 25 April 1794 present: Archelaus Hughes, Abraham Penn, James Lyon, Brett Stovall, Jonathan Hanby, Edward Tatum.
-Hall vs Amos, George Penn added to reference
-Wingo vs Vest, John Sharp Spl Bl, next Court
-John Cameron is appointed surveyor of the road from the banks of the Mayo at the mouth of Penns lane to James Taylors in place of Taylor.
-Crouch vs Pulliam
-Beveridge Hughes is to appear at the next Court to give testamony relative to the last will of Cornelius Deweese dec'd.
Jury: Josiah Farris foreman, George Rogers Sr, John Sharp, John Crum, Peter France, Nathaniel N. Helton, Richard Davison, William Gray, Augustine Thomas, Jacob Adams Sr, George Rogers Jr, James Ferrell and William Deal.
-Saunders vs Tuggle
-Hall vs Jones: depo of Lewis Burris, Francis McCraw, Hugh Armstrong and James Brison Jr to be taken.
-Breden Jr vs Mankin, Joseph Newman a garnishee being served saith he owes the Defendant nothing..dismissed. Also on another garnishee served, saith the same.
-Edward Tatum, Brett Stovall, Augustine Thomas, Jacob Critz and William Smith are appointed Commissioners.
-Koger vs Shelton
-McGee vs Charles
-Deed- Abraham Penn to George Hairston
-Lyon vs Scott
-Allen vs Pipes, jury sworn: Woody Burge, John Mankin, Daniel Adams, John Medley, William McPeak, Henry McGuffey, David Morgan, Richard Vest, Nathaniel Smith, Robert Taylor, Eliphaz Shelton. Verdict for Pltf.
-John Jones 2 days witness for William Allen vs Philip Pipes
-John Allen 2 days for same

PAGE 65

COURT April 1794 present: Archelaus Hughes, Abraham Penn, James Lyon, Charles Thomas, James Armstrong, George Penn, Brett Stovall, Jonathan Hanby, Edward Tatum.
-Hairston vs Redmond, jury sworn: Stephen Senter, William Allen, Golder Davison, Soloman Stephens, Jeremiah Burnett, Frederick Fitzgerald, Drury Soloman, John Jones, Stephen Jones, Pierce Guinn, William Fitzgerald, Joseph Going. Verdict for Pltf.
-McCrery & Wallace vs Griffin, jury sworn: James Taylor, Joseph Newman, Humphrey Smith, William James Mayo, ~~William Adams~~, William McPeak, Thomas Hall, David Morgan, John Hall, Henry McGuffey and Drury Soloman.
-Deed- Hugh Armstrong to John Walters
-Amos vs Hall -Hall vs Amos
-Robert Rowen assignee of George Brooks produced in Court an account for 12 days guarding the County Jail.
-Humphrey Smith 3 days witness William Amos vs N. Hall
-Henry Koger, leave is granted him to keep an Ordinary in the town of Taylorsville, A. Hughes his security.
-Charles Smith 2 days and 25 miles witness William Griffin vs McCrery & Wallace.

Page 65 contd

COURT 26 April 1794 present: Abraham Penn, James Lyon, Gabriel Penn, Edward Tatum.
-Pennington vs Polson
-Napier vs Amoss
-Kimzey vs Gee
-Grand Jury returned and made several presentments.
-Joyce vs Lyon
-Hampton vs Johnson & Boyd
-Sumpter vs Reaves
-Staples vs Shelton
-Joyce vs Lyon

PAGE 66

-Tanner vs Rowan, jury sworn: William James Mayo, John Sharp, Noah Parr, William Keaton, Robert Litrell, Joseph H. Duvall, Robert Sharp, John Tatum, Charles Vest, Charles Sutton, Woody Burge, Eliphaz Shelton. verdict for Pltf.
-Corn vs Oldham
-J. Penn vs Carlin
-G. Penn vs Carlin
-Staples vs Parr
-Dickerson vs Maberry, not guilty
-John Clark 3 days witness William Tanner vs R. Rowan
-Robert Taylor 3 days same
-Hairston vs Cornwell
-Gabriel Penn, Jailor for the County produced an account for sundry services.
-Thomas Mitchell same
-Samuel Staples same
-Thomas Mitchell produced 3 lists of insolvents for year of 1791.
COURT Thursday 29 April 1794 present: Archelaus Hughes, James Lyon, Gabriel Penn, Samuel Clark, John Breden Jr
-Deed- Amos Rowark to Joshua Hall
-Deed- John Poteet to Jesse Corn
-Deed- Saphaniah Tenison to William Bristoe
-Phillip Buzzard is exempt from the payment of County and Parish levies for the future.
-Account current of the estate of Nathan Going dec'd returned
-Deed- Mayo Carrington attorney in fact for Richard Adams to John Burnett
-same to Zachariah Burnett and Micajah Burnett
-same to Nathaniel Ross
-same to Thomas Mitchell
-Deed- William Amoss to David Harbour Sr.
-William & Garland vs Philpott, dismissed

PAGE 67

-William Sneed is appointed surveyor of the road from the forks of the road above Silas Ratliff to the Bull Mtn Rd by B. Foley.
-William Adams is appointed surveyor of the road from the ford of Spoon Creek above Hamon Critz to the line posts in place of William Fain.
-John Jones (school master) is exempt from the payment of County and Parish levies for the future.
-Staples vs Parr: dedimus awarded Pltf to take depo of Charles Farris andWinney his daughter.
-Moore vs Shelton, Pltf to take depo of Joshua Nelson and A. Shelton of Stokes Co N.C.. Joseph Cloud, John Martin, Charles Beasley, James Martin, William Bates and George Deatheridge gentlemen appointed Commissioners for this matter.
-Also take depo of David Humphreys in the County of Surry, N.C., James Brison, Martin Armstrong, Andrew Kencannon, John Donigan, John Jackson, Samuel Humphreys, Henry Herring, gentlemen appointed Commissioners.
-Deed- David Going to William Nolen
-George Penn produced a certificate from the Governor appointing him Lt. Col. of the Militia in this County, took usual oaths.
-Stephen Lyon qualified as Major of 1st Btn

Page 67 contd

-Jesse Corn, John Poteet, Jacob Critz, John Parr qualified as Captains of the Militia.
-Samuel Staples produced a Commission appointing him Captain of a Company of Riflemen of the 2nd Btn.
-John Hanby qualified as Lt.
-John Frances as Lt. of a company of riflemen
-William Sharp, James Turner, George Lackey as Lts.
-Elijah Banks recommended as Ensign of Riflemen in the 1st Btn.
-John Hays as Ensign 1st Btn of Militia
-Samuel Clark Jr same
-John Turner same
-Martin Dickinson as Ensign of 2nd Btn
-Thomas Whitlock appointed Lt of 2nd Btn
-Nathaniel Smith same
-Josiah Farris appointed Lt of the 1st Btn
-On a motion of Charles Vest, it is the opinion of the Court that an outside chimney be used for the Courthouse, the cost to be ascertained by Samuel Shelton.

PAGE 68

May Court 1794
-Nancy Lyon widow and relict of Humberston Lyon relinquishes her right of dower and claims a childs part.
-Edward Lewis appeared in Court and was examined touching his wounds received in the late Wars and it is the opinion of this Court that his pension be continued.
-Adkinson vs Scott
-On a motion of Mathew Moore judgment is granted him vs Amos Rowark and John Christian.
-Ordered that the executors of Wright vs Innis be stayed
-Last will and testament of Cornelius Deweese, executor refused to act.
COURT Thursday 26 June 1794 present: Samuel Clark, John Breden Jr, James Lyon, William Banks
-Deed of gift William Willmouth to Mary Turner
-Deed- Isaac Adams to Brett Stovall
-Deed- Mayo Carrington attorney for Richard Adams to Zachariah Burnett and Micajah Burnett
-Deed- same to Thomas Mitchell - further proved
-George Fulcher allowed 6 days guarding County Jail and Thomas Garrison.
-Brett Stovall qualified as Lt of Militia
-Charles Hibbert as Ensign of Militia
-Henry Smith as Captain
-Deed- Charles Hibberts to John Going
-James Lyon Jr qualified as Lt of Militia

PAGE 69

-On the motion of Gabriel Penn leave is granted him to keep an Ordinary at the Courthouse, Robert Rowan his security
-William Banks gentleman, appointed to receive the monies subscribed in the County of Henry and Patrick under an Act of Assembly for clearing and extending the navigation of the Roan Oak River, appeared in Court with Samuel Staples and Samuel Clark his security.
-Stephen vs Elkins
-Bolling vs Bolling
-Amos vs Stephens
-Laurance vs Bryd
-Gibson vs Polson
-Smith vs Kimzey
-Baker vs Griffin
-Gibson vs Hooker
-Adkinson vs Bryd
-Moore vs Shelton
-Jesse Corn allowed 4 days witness Soloman Stephens vs M. Amos
-James Morrison 5 days for same
-Lawson vs Rowan
-Dewit vs Douglas
-Cockran vs Philpott
-Dickerson vs Adkinson
-Pennington vs Bristoe
-Rowark vs Jones
-Dewit vs Hall
-Baker vs Walter
-Dodson vs Brown

Page 69 contd

-Johnson vs Senter, dedimus to take depo of Elizabeth Johnson and John Johnson.

PAGE 70

COURT July 31, 1794 present: Archelaus Hughes, William Banks, Charles Foster, Gabriel Penn, Francis Turner, John Breden Jr.
-Saunders vs Burnett
-Deed- Augustine Thomas to Hannah Mayo
-Deed- James Shard to James Fulkerson
-Commonwealth vs Burnett
-Deed- Charles Collier to Humphrey Posey
-Archelaus Hughes Jr recommended as Deputy Surveyor, to be examined by Humphrey Smith.
-Hairston vs Staples, Ignatious Redman, Spl Bl
-James Taylor foreman, Stephen Senter, William Allen, William Hancock, Beveridge Hughes, Thomas Harbour, Moses Reynolds, George Penn, Thomas Hollandsworth, Joel Chitwood, James Thompson, Arthur Parr, William Deal, Charles Rakes, William Keaton and John Burnett to serve as Grand Jury.
-Overseers of the Poor to bind out Jenny Litten to Henry Koger
-Administration of the estate of Abraham Bird dec'd granted to Samuel Kennon with John Ross his security
-...... vs Tuggle
-Munford Smith, David Rowark, John Christian, Bartlett Smith to appraise the estate of Abraham Bird.
-William Carter qualified as Major of the Militia
-Joseph Stovall, Charles Foster and Munford Smith as Captains
-Robert Hudspeth as Lieutenant
-Commonwealth vs Sundries on presentments at April Court are dismissed for reasons appearing to this Court
-Grand Jury returned several sentiments
-Rowan vs Clark, William Deal Spl Bl

PAGE 71

July Court, present: A. Hughes, James Lyon, Francis Turner, Charles Thomas, James Armstrong, William Banks, William Carter, Gabriel Penn, Edward Tatum, Brett Stovall, Munford Smith, John Breden Jr, Joseph Stovall and Charles Foster.
-Daniel Carlin, Jonathan Hanby and Samuel Clark are recommended as fit persons to serve as Sheriff.
-James Poteet Jr produced a commission appointing him Ensign of the Militia
-Koger vs Shelton
-Tatum vs Mankin, on an attachment, Henry A. Dean a garnishee being sworn saith he owes the Defendant one mans saddle which was formerly condemned to satisfy and order sale brought by Eliphaz Shelton against said Defendant and it is ordered that the surplus of the said saddle if any, be sold according to Law to satisfy present attachment.
-Lyne vs Gardner, William Willmouth Spl Bl
-Walter vs Ogle
-Burnett vs Mayos executors on an attachment Judgment, Joseph Reynolds a garnishee says he owes Defendant sufficient to satisfy Pltf.

PAGE 72

COURT July 1794 present: William Banks, Francis Turner, Gabriel Penn and Brett Stovall.
-Deed- Joseph Johnson to Daniel Barnard
-Deed- Henry Sumpter to George Reaves
-McCrery & Wallace vs Griffin
-Stephens vs Stults
-James Griffin 4 days witness William Guinn vs McCrery and Wallace
-Francis vs Going
-Jones vs Hall

-Pennington vs Polson, jury sworn: Joseph Johnson, Henry Koger, John Medley, Samuel Shelton, John Wallace, Thomas Morrow, George Stults, William Deal, Robert Hudspeth, Miller Easley, Woody Burge, John Fletcher..verdict for Pltf.
-Lyon vs Adams on an attachment John Adams a garnishee being sworn said he owes Defd nothing, dismissed.
-Napier vs Amos
-Lyon vs Scott
-Hampton vs Johnson
-Kimzey vs Gee
-Joyce vs Lyon
-Sumpter vs Reaves
-Edward Tatum appeared in Court and qualified Taxalbe property for year of 1794.
-Maberry Jr for the benefit of George Hairston vs Thomas Gee
-Staples vs Shelton
-Penn vs Carlin
-Staples vs Parr
-Allen vs Allen
-Corn vs Oldham
-Dickerson vs Maberry Jr
-Hairston vs Cornwell
-Deed- Michael Cloer to George Hairston

PAGE 73

-Turman vs Hairston
-Hall vs Price, jury sworn: John Medley, Thomas Morrow, William Deal, Robert Hudspeth, Miller Easley, Woody Burge, John Fletcher, Isaac Dodson, Noah Parr, Henry Tuggle, Charles Vest, Samuel Dalton.verdict for Pltf in amount of one penny.
-Edward Tatum gentleman, Commissioner presented an account for 1794 in the amount of $70.00.
-Deed- Stephen Lyon to James McCain
-Lyon vs Scott, jury sworn: John Medley, Thomas Morrow, William Deal, Robert Hudspeth, Miller Easley, Woody Burge, John Fletcher, Isaac Dodson, Noah Parr, Henry Tuggle, Charles Vest, Samuel Dalton.
-Martin Amos vs Gabriel Penn
-John Bowen ? 3 days witness Isaac Pennington vs Andrew Polson
-Barberry Griffin 1 day witness William Griffin vs William Scott
-Rowan vs Baker, Eliphaz Shelton Spl Bl
-Boyd vs Killey
-Thomas Jett 1 day 35 miles witness for Noah Parr vs Samuel Staples
-Lyon vs Smith
-Hairston vs Slater
-Mc Alexander vs McPeak
-Webb vs Shelton
-Charles Farris 1 day 25 miles witness Samuel Staples vs Noah Parr
-Robert Hudspeth qualified as Overseer of the Poor
-Rebeckah Morrow 1 day witness Jesse Corn vs Thomas Oldham
-Ordered that a Ducking Stool be made for use of the County
-Thomas Morrow, John Davenport, James Morrison, Betsy Morrison are each allowed 1 day witness Jesse Corn vs Thomas Oldham.
-Moore vs Going
-Deed- William Adams to Samuel Packwood

PAGE 74

COURT Thursday 28 August 1794 present: Archelaus Hughes, William Banks, Gabriel Penn, Hamon Critz, Charles Thomas, Brett Stovall.
-Deed- William Seaife and wife to Caleb Flawid
-Deed of Gift- Arch. Hughes to Levy Hughes and Archelaus Hughes
-Deed- Samuel Perry to John Ingram
-Deed- George Hairston to Charles Rakes
-Deed- Peter Donovan to George Hairston
-Deed- Luke Foley to Jacob Saunders
-Deed- Joseph Johnson to Joseph Jackson
-Deed- William Hudspeth to Carter Hudspeth
-Deed- Nathan Hall to the heirs of William Tharp
-Deed- James Poteet Jr to Jesse Corn
-Deed- William Isham to Luke Foley
-Thomas Bristoe appointed surveyor of the road from Charles Fosters to the Franklin line in place of Benjamin Mize
-On a petition of the inhabitants of the North Mayo for a review of a road, it is ordered that Philip Penn, Josiah Farris, Peter France and Jacob Critz or 3 of them view a way for a road from the layne of John Cameron and report.

Page 74 contd

-William Perkins Sr appeared in Court with Nathan Hall his security, posted Bond and is to be of good behavior towards Sally Lemmon ? for 2 months 1 day.
-Humphrey Smith qualified as executor of the LW&T of Cornelius Deweese dec'd. Nathan Hall his security.
-On a motion of Daniel Carlin gentleman sheriff of this County, John Tatum is admitted as Deputy.
-John Burnett, Zachariah Burnett, Micajah Burnett and William Fuson or any 3 to appraise the estate of Cornelius Deweese dec'd.
-Inventory and account of the estate of Ab. Bird returned
-Humphrey vs Griffin, Pltf take depo of David Humphreys.

PAGE 75

August Court 1794
-William Nowling appointed surveyor of the road from Jacob Adams Jr to the South Mayo in place of Lot Litrall.
-Ordered that Charles Thomas, Esquire, take into his hands the papers of John Henderson dec'd and deliver them to the next Court.
-Dodson vs Brown
-Deed- John Renn to Moses Reynolds
-Stephens vs Elkins
-Bolling vs Bolling
-John Norton 2 days 28 miles witness Benjamin Philpott vs William Cockaran.
-Smith vs Poteet to be determined by David Morgan, James Bartlett and William Sharp or any two of them.
-Archelaus Hughes qualified as Deputy Surveyor
-Deed of Trust- John Breden Jr to George Penn Jr in favor of Trent and Briscoe.
-Gardner vs Hughes, Martin Amoss a garnishee saith he owes the Defdt sufficient to satisfy the Pltf.
-Pennington vs Bristoe
-N.P. Lawless vs Washington
-Lyne vs Kimzey

PAGE 76

COURT Friday 29 August 1794 present: Archelaus Hughes, James Lyon, Abraham Penn, William Banks
-Baker vs Griffin
-Gibson vs Hooker
-Adkinson vs Boyd
-Moore vs Dove
-Dugan vs Killey
-Gibson vs Hooker
-Laurence vs Boyd
-Gibson vs Polson
-Carlin vs Boyd
-Lawson vs Bowman
-Deed- Rhodham Litrell to Eliphaz Shelton, Hanah Litrell wife of Rhodham Litrell relinquishes her right of dower.
-Dewit vs Dougless
-Cockran vs Philpott
-Baker vs Walter
-Dewit vs Hall
-Rowark vs Jones
-Dickerson vs Adkinson
-McCrery & Wallace vs Quillin
-Jonathan Hanby 2 days witness Jacob Lawson vs Robert Rowan
-Robert Hall 3 days for same
-Penn vs Garrett
-Hall vs Breden N.P.
-Ordered that Edward Tatum, Esquire, to purchase a record book suitable for deeds,etc. The Sheriff to pay for same.
-Lyne vs Gardner
-David Hanby appointed surveyor of the road from the forks of the road below Edward Tatum to where the said road from this Courthouse comes into the Hollow Rd in place of Agustine Brown.
-William Smith appointed surveyor of the road from the forks of the road above Stephen Lyon to Peters Creek in Hanbys Lane.

PAGE 77

COURT Thursday 25 September 1795 present: Abraham Penn, William Banks, Charles Thomas, Brett Stovall, Charles Foster, John Breden Jr.
-Deed- Harris Carter to James Lyon
-Deed- James Mankin to Samuel Waggoner
-Deed- William Scarife and wife to Peter Simmons
-Deed- Abraham Penn to James Lyon
-Power of attorney of William Wells to John Clark
-Deed- George Dodson Sr to Jesse Dodson
-Deed- George Dodson Sr to Leonard Dodson
-Deed- Michael Litrell to Thomas Willis
-Deed- William Fain to John Botetourt
-On the motion of William Preston Skillern and James Risque,gentlemen leave is granted them to practice Law at this Court.
-Smith vs Poteet, depo of Dun Solyears and James Dodson to be taken.
-Henry H. Dean, James Dickerson, John Jackson, Stephen Senter or any 3 to view a way for a road from near Collin Hamptons to the top of the Good Spur at the Grayson line and report.
-A view of a report of a road from out of Bull Mtn to this Courthouse returned.
-Harvey Fitzgerald appointed surveyor of the road from the top of Bull Mtn to this Courthouse in place of George Stults.
-Ordered that Eliphaz Shelton with his hands call on George Fulchers hands and Harvey Fitzgerald and his list and that they clear and open a road out of the Bull Mtn to this Courthouse.
-Deed- Martin Simms to Joshua Adams (2)
-Administration of the estate of John Henderson dec'd granted George Hairston with Charles Thomas his security.
-Deed- Edmond Brammer to Hugh Boyd
-Charles Thomas, Charles Foster, William Fuson, John Koger or any 3 to appraise the estate of John Henderson dec'd.

PAGE 78

-Deed of Trust, Hamon Frans to Gabriel Penn
-Bill of Sale, John Abington to Bowls Abington
-Mary Renn wife of John Renn relinquishes her right of dower in a deed to Moses Reynolds.
-Medley vs Hale
-Stephen Lyon came into Court and objects to the validity of a conveyance this day made by James Mankins to Samuel Waggoner.
-John Koger appointed Commissioner to value property in place of John Henderson.
-Power of attorney of Joshua Adams to Daniel Adams
-Thomas Mitchell appointed Collector in the County of Washington for taxes years of 1782,83,84 under an act passed 26 Dec 1792. Entitled an Act to provide more effectual for the collection of the publick in certain cases; together with William Mitchell, Daniel Carlin, William Griffin, James Lyon and Edward Tatum his securities for the collection of the Revenue Tax for the years 1782-83,84 and also for the Cert.Tax for 1783 and 1784.
-George Fulcher Sr appointed surveyor of the road from the line past below this place to this Court in place of Nathan Litrell.
-Jesse Tatum is admitted Deputy Sheriff under Daniel Carlin Sheriff.

-Hooker	vs Gibson	-Lawrence	vs Boyd
-Adkinson	vs Boyd	-Gibson	vs Polson
-Moore	vs Dove	-Carlin	vs Boyd
-Dugan	vs Killey	-Dewitt	vs Douglas
-Dewitt	vs Hall	-Cockran	vs Philpott

-Power of attorney of William Scott. Sarah Scott, Henry Blancett,Nancy Blancett, Joshua Hains, Elizabeth Hains, to William Griffin.
-John Norton 1 day and 28 miles witness Benjamin Philpott vs William Cockaran.

-Rowark	vs Jones	-Humphrey	vs Griffin

PAGE 79

COURT Friday 26 September 1794 present: Abraham Penn, Samuel Clark, Gabriel Penn, Edward Tatum.
-Ordered that the poor orphans of Cornelius Deweese be bound out by the Overseers of the Poor.
-Samuel Clark Jr Commissioned as Ensign of the Militia
-Charles Foster, John Koger, William Sharp and William Fuson or any 3 of them to lay off and allot to Barberry Foley, widow and relict of Barthalomew Foley 1/3 part of his lands and make report and divide the real and personal estate amongst his heirs.
-Baker vs Walters
-Lyne vs Kimzey
-Lawless vs Washington
-Birds Adm. vs Freeman
-Smith vs Poteet
-Baker vs Griffin
-Hall vs Breden Jr
-Hairston vs Newman
-Pennington vs Bristoe
-Hairston vs Cornwell
-Smith vs Read
-Smith vs King
-Hairston vs Stratton
-Smith, attorney in fact for William Gilliam vs D. Mullins
-John Tatum qualified as Ensign of the Militia

PAGE 80

COURT Thursday 30 October 1794 present: Archelaus Hughes, Samuel Clark, Francis Turner, Joseph Stovall
-Deed- James Denny to John Henry, Esther Denny wife of James Denny relinquishes her right of dower.
-Deed- Tandy Senter to John Davis
-Deed- William Mills to Richard Mills
-Deed- Charles Collier to John Smallman
-Nathaniel Smith and Thomas Whitlock commissioned as Lieutenants of the Militia.
-Deed- Charles Foster attorney in fact for Bennett Posey to Harrison Hubbert.
-Deed- Harrison Hubbert to Moses Godward
COURT present: James Lyon, William Banks, Charles Foster, Munford Smith, Brett Stovall, John Breden Jr.
-Edward Tatum is continued as a Commissioner for this County.
-Harrison Hubbert and Thomas Whitlock are recommended as fit and proper persons to serve as Commissioners of the Peace.
-Deed- Charles Foster attorney in fact for Bennett Posey to Richard Baker.
-Deed- Richard Baker to Joseph Commings
-Lawson vs Rogers
-Danger vs Fry and others
-John Nunns produced credentials of his being in regular communion with the Baptitst Society, his security James Lyon.
-Dean vs Smith
-An instrument of writing under the hands of William Bobbet and Nathaniel Pops?? were presented in Court by John Hammond and recorded.
-John Breden foreman, James Taylor, William Sharp, Arthur Parr, Stephen Senter, William Allen, Stephen Jones, Bethany Haines, Beveridge Hughes, John Hall, George Rogers Jr, Thomas Willis, James Ferrell, Joel Chitwood, William Hancock and John Crum are appointed as Grand Jury for this County.
-William Carter,Samuel Clark, Charles Foster and Brett Stovall are appointed Commissioners of the Court to receive the Courthouse and make a report thereof to the Court, or any three of them.
-Blankenship vs Chitwood, William Willis Spl Bl.
-On a motion of Eliphaz Shelton leave is granted him to build a grist mill on the South Mayo River.

PAGE 81

-Smith vs Poteet
-Grand Jury returned to Court and made several presentments.
-Lackey vs Breden, referred to Thomas Goodson, Samuel Eason, A. Penn, Samuel Staples, David Morgan and Charles Thomas.
-Smith vs Grimmet, Andrew Polson a garnishee sworn saith he owes the

Page 81 contd

the Defendant nothing.
-On a motion of Ann Banks by her attorney, it is ordered that the former order of this Court relative to the appointment of William Banks to take into his possession the estate of the said Ann Banks is rescinded. Ordered that Samuel Croucher, William Banks and Joseph Stovall to take the said estate as Trustees.
COURT 1 October 1794 present: Arch. Hughes, James Lyon, Charles Thomas, Brett Stovall, John Breden Jr, Francis Turner.
-Breden vs Lackey, take the deposition of William McNeley, Rebecca McNeley and daughter Rebecca, John Martin and wife, Jane Martin, Hasa Martin, Polly Martin and Sally Martin.
-Samuel Staples vs Eliphaz Shelton guardian for Easop Shelton, Abigail Shelton, Liberty Shelton, Mary Shelton and also Abram Penn attorney in fact for Ralph Shelton, Palitiah Shelton, Jeremiah Shelton, William McGehe, Julious Roberson, Dudley Rutherford, William Jones, William Arnold, Roger Shelton, Azariah Shelton, Ezekiah Shelton and James Shelton heirs of Ralph Shelton dec'd Defendants. The Defendants not having appeared it is ordered that George Carter, Edward Tatum, Nathaniel Smith, William Smith Jr and David Hanby are appointed Commissioners to lay off and divide the land named in the Complaint.
-Jacob Ayrs 2 days witness McCreary & Wallace vs Griffin
-Elihu Ayrs 2 days for same
-On the motion of Ann Banks by her attorney that the order of the Court yesterday relative to the appointment of Trustees to take the estate devised to her by her deceased husband be rescinded and that Joseph Stovall and Brett Stovall are appointed.
-Power of attorney of James Armstrong to Munford Smith
-Power of attorney of Bennett Posey to Charles Foster

PAGE 82

-Breden and wife vs Ruble and wife, Pltf to take depo of Chistian Geig? and Mary Lemmon ??.
-same vs same take depo of James Mitchell and James Turner
-James Lyon to convey titles to purchasers of lots sold in the town of Taylorsville upon the purchasers paying up their balance.
-Adams vs Lyon
-Rowark vs Jones
-Commonwealth vs Ross
-same vs Guin
-same vs Maberry Jr
-McCrery & Wallace vs Griffin, jury sworn: Nathaniel Smith, David Rogers, Jesse Corn, Terry Hughes, Elisha Harbour, William Easley, Stephen Senter, Martin Amoss, William Hickinbottom, George Carter, Frederick Fitzgerald, Major Hancock..verdict for Pltf.
-A report of Gentlemen Commissioners appointed for inspecting the Courthouse reported that they received the same.
-Elisabeth Gardner relinquishes her right of dower in a deed conveyed to George Hairston by her husband.
-Kimzey vs Gee
-Staples vs Shelton
-Penn vs Carlin
-Sumpter vs Reaves
-Corn vs Oldham
-Hairston vs Stratton on a atta. Bartlett Smith a garnishee being sworn saith he owes the Defd nothing.
-Dickerson vs Maberry Jr
-Staples vs Parr-
-Smith vs Isbill, to take depo of Rueben George
-David McGown appointed Constable in place of Job Ross.
-John Oldham 3 days 38 miles witness for Thomas Oldham
-Rebecca Morrow 1 day for same
-Jane Morrison 1 day for same
-Elisabeth Morrison 1 day for same
-Thomas Morrison 1 day for same
-Charles Smith,Esquire, 1 day 25 miles witness William Griffin vs McCrery & Wallace.
-John Gittons 2 days for same
-Killey vs Boyd

Page 82 contd

-Boyd vs Killey referred to Munford Smith, William Carter, James Dickerson and Thomas Whitlock or any 3.
-William Berry 2 days witness for McCrery vs Griffin.

PAGE 83

-James Shelton and wife against Easop Shelton, Abigail Shelton, Liberty Shelton, Mary Shelton, Ralph Shelton, Palitiah Shelton, Jeremiah Shelton, William McGehe, Julious Roberson, Dudley Rutherford, William Arnold, William Jones, Roger Shelton, Azeriah Shelton, Ezekiah Shelton, Eliphaz Shelton, heirs of Ralph Shelton dec'd Defendants. The Defendants waving all errors and not gain saying the claim of Complainants. It is ordered that the land according to the Poayer of said Bill be decreed to them.
-Rowan vs Brown, defendant take depo of Obediah Binge?Burge? and Hugh Armstrong.
COURT Saturday 1 November 1794 present: Arch. Hughes, William Carter, Brett Stovall, John Breden Jr.
-Deed- Michael Killey to John Yeates
-James Shelton and wife Susannah to Samuel Staples, a Deed.
-On the motion of William Griffin by his attorney for an injunction to stay the proceedings of a judgement obtained by McCrery & Wallace.
-Staples vs Parr, jury sworn: John Clark, William Deal, John Walter, William Hickinbottom, George Carter, William McCrery, Joseph H. Duvall, Henry Harrison Dean, William France, Terry Hughes, Golder Davison, Charles Sutton.
-Abijah Hughes 4 days witness Noah Parr vs Samuel Staples
-T. Hughes vs William France
-William Carter, Jonathan Hanby, Edward Tatum and James Taylor or any 3 appointed to lay off and allot the widow and relict of Ralph Shelton dec'd of the residue of land of which Ralph Shelton died seized of after deducting J. Shelton and wifes claim.
-Senter vs Johnson, jury sworn: George Stults, John Bolt, John Hanby, Richard Adkinson, Nathaniel Smith, William Griffin, Noah Parr, Gabriel Penn, William Cornwell, Jacob Dean, Jesse Corn and John Boyd. Vereict returned for each party to pay his own costs.
-Elijah Banks 2 days witness John Clark vs R. Rowan
-Deed of Trust John Sharp to Eliphaz Shelton
-Thomas Jett 2 days 35 miles witness Noah Parr vs Samuel Staples
-Jacob Dean 2 days 40 miles for same

PAGE 84

-Charles Stewart allowed 2 days witness Terry Hughes vs William France
-Brown vs Rowan
-Clark vs Rowan
-Baker vs Rowan
-Hughes vs France, Pltf to take depo of Charles Stewart
-Major Hancock 2 days witness Jesse Corn vs John Bolt
-John Davenport 2 days for same
-John Jones 3 days witness Tandy Senter vs Joseph Johnson
-William Allen 3 days for same
-William Bucknall 3 days for same
-Corn vs Bolt referred to James Poteet Jr, John Poteet, William Gardner, John Koger or any three of them.
-Corn vs Oldham, same as above
--Jacob Baker allowed 5 days witness
-Charles Vest 5 days witness
-Samuel Staples 5 days witness
-John Hanby allowed 2 days witness John Clark vs Robert Rowan
-Samuel Staples 2 days for same
COURT Thursday 27 November 1794 present: Charles Thomas, Hamon Critz, Edward Tatum, Brett Stovall, John Breden Jr, Joseph Stovall
-Deed- Thomas Garrison to John Tuggle
-Smith vs McGehe
-Deed- Richard Adams to Jacob Critz
-Deed- Thomas Hill to Jacob Critz

Page 84 contd

-Deed- George Stults to James McCain
-Deed- William Isham to Mathew Morrow
-Lewis vs Perkins
-William Fuson appointed Constable in place of Thomas Bristoe
-Smith vs Poteet Jr
-Report of a view of a road thru the land of John Cameron returned
-Hairston vs Daniel Newman
-Deed- Joshua Hudson to Edward Tatum
-A lien for a term of years from Shadrack Barrett to Joseph Going

PAGE 85

-Deed- Samuel Noe to Benjamin Hancock
-Daniel Newman is exempt from paying levies for the future
-Gibson vs Hooker
-Laurance vs James Boyd
-Deed- Peter Dunavan to George Hairston
-Thomas Roe Hall recommended as Ensign of Militia in place of James Poteet Jr.
-Thomas Whitlock recommended as Captain in place of William Griffin
-Martin Dickerson recommended as Lieutenant
-Benjamin Cloud as Ensign
-Hall vs Breden Sr
-Davison vs Lanier
COURT Friday 28 November present: Edward Tatum, Charles Thomas, Brett Stovall, John Breden Jr
-Gibson vs Polson
-Dugan vs Killey
-Dewit vs Hall
-Lyne vs Kimzey
-Lawson vs Washington
-Hairston vs Cornwell
-Cole vs Rowark
-Lindsay vs Keaton
-Shelton vs Garrott
-Shelton vs Barrott
-Dodson vs Brown
-Carlin vs Boyd
-Dewitt vs Douglass
-Baker vs Walters
-Pennington vs Bristoe
-Wilson for Hairston vs J. Newman
-Baker vs Griffin
-Branham vs Helton
-Corn vs Bolt
-Hairston vs Stratton
-Shelton vs Mankin
-Fulden? Smith for George Hairston vs Joseph Newman, dismissed

PAGE 86

-Lyon vs Adams
-Pigg vs Harrold
-Shelton vs McCain
-Charles Thomas 1 day witness Nathan Hall vs John Breden Jr
-Armstrong vs Cody

The County for the year 1794	
Sheriff for annual salary	25.
Clerk for same	25.
Deputy States Attorney for same	25.
Thomas Mitchell for Henry France for one old wolf head	4.17
	79.17

COURT Thursday 25 December 1794 present James Lyon, William Banks, Jonathan Hanby, Edward Tatum, Hamon Critz.
-Power of attorney of William Griffin Jr to Joseph Griffin
-Hornsby vs Hensley
-Saunders vs Martin
-Edward Tatum, Jonathan Hanby and Nathaniel Smith or two of them to settle the accounts current of Nathan Going, dec'd.
-Deed- Joshua Hudson to Edward Tatum
-Deed- Samuel Noe and wife to Benjamin Hancock
-Deed- Richard Adams to Jacob Critz
-Deed- Thomas Hill to Jacob Critz
-Deed- George Maberry Sr and George Maberry Jr to David Morgan

Page 86 contd

-Deed- George Stults to James McCain
-Deed- Benjamin Butterworth to William Burnett
-William Carter and James Lyon appointed to inspect and review if they think proper the stocks and pillory for theCounty and report.
-Lackey vs Breden
-Deed- Thomas Gazaway to Harvey Fitzgerald - 2 deeds, Anney Gazaway wife of Thomas relinquishes her right of dower
-Benjamin Garrett appointed surveyor of the road from the forks below A. Hudsons to the top of the mountain.
-Deed- Joshua Hudson to Robert Hall

PAGE 87
-Ordered that the Sheriff advertise that there will be an election held at the house of John Koger onthe first Monday in April next and that Charles Foster do superintend the said election within the former District for theNortheast side of the Bull Mtn and also elect the same day at the house of Samuel Clark for the Lower District on the south-west side of the said mountain and that Archelaus Hughes do superintend same, the election for the Overseer of the Poor.
-Deed- Joshua Hudson to Golder Davison
-List of insolvent tithes due Thomas Mitchell Deputy Sheriff for William Mitchell for the year 1792 were presented.
-List for the year 1793 for Daniel Carlin Sheriff also presented.
-Pigg vs Herrald
COURT Thursday 29 January 1795 present: James Lyon, Gabriel Penn, Edward Tatum, John Breden Jr, Jonathan Hanby, William Carter.
-On the motion of Detherick Yoes leave is granted him to keep an Ordinary at his house together with Joseph R. Johnson his security.
-Shelton vs Garrett
-Noah Parr is appointed surveyor of the road from the South Mayo to Spoon Creek in place of George Corn.
-Ordered that the road from the forks above Shadrick Barretts to the forks below David Hanbys leading by James Sheltons be discontinued.
-Adams vs Going
-Gibson vs Hooker
-Carlin vs Boyd
-Dewitt vs Douglass
-Pennington vs Bristoe
-Cole vs Rowark
-Shelton vs Mankin
-Armstrong vs Cody
-Call vs Street
-Laurence vs Boyd
-Adkinson vs Boyd
-Dugan vs Killey
-Dewitt vs Hall
-Baker vs Griffin
-Hairston vs Keaton
-Gilliam vs Mullings
-Branham vs Helton
-Fontaines Adm vs Hammons Jr

PAGE 88

-Lackey vs Breden and son
-Dickerson vs Maberry Jr
-Breden and wife vs Ruble and wife, depo of James Turner, James Mitchell and George Dudley be taken.
-same vs same, take depositon of Christian Grigg, Mary Lemon, Thomas Hale, Isaah Willis, Samuel Hairston and Polley James.
-same vs same, deposition of Thomas Baker, Robert Baker, Samuel Wood, James Carr Sr, James Carr Jr, Gilbert Strayhorne and wife, John Tinnin and wife be taken.
-McCrery & Wallace vs Griffin
-Samuel Staples vs Griffin
-William Nowlin appointed surveyor of the road from Jacob Adams Jr to the Patrick Courthouse
-Francis vs Going, take deposition of Jacob Lawson
-Detherick Yois appointed surveyor of the road from Woods Gap to the Carolina line above Bakers shop.
-Harvey Fitzgerald appointed Constable in place of Jacob Lawson.

Page 88 contd

COURT Thursday 26 February 1795 present: Arch. Hughes, Samuel Clark, Francis Turner, William Banks, Edward Tatum, John Breden Jr.
-Deed- Henry Sumpter to George Reaves, Agge wife of Henry Sumpter relinquishes her right of dower
-Deed- James Ferrell to Mesheck Perdue
-Deed- Garland Akin to Richard Stone
-Deed- John Parr Sr to Robert Crump
-Deed- John Botetourt to Cornelius Keaton, Anny Botetourt relinquishes her right of dower
-Deed of Gift Frederick Fulkerson to James ______
-Deed- Stephen Senter to Mitchell Thompson and Catherine Thompson
-Deed- Stephen Senter to Uriah McMillian
-Deed- William Isom to Isham Burnett
-Deed- Edward Tatum to William Lawson
-Deed- Moses Reynolds to Samuel Croucher
-Also Zachariah Burnett a relinquishment of his claim intwo certain tracts of land toMicajah Burnett proved.

PAGE 89

-Deed- Peter Stolts to William Allen
-Deed- Thomas Oldham to James Ferrell
-Deed- Aaron Walden to Edward Lewis
-Ordered that the Overseers of the Poor bind out Selahard...? to James Thompson
-James Taylor foreman, Nathaniel N. Helton, Miller W. Easley, Robert Hall, William Easley, Woody Burge, Leonard Dodson, John Randals, John Miller, John Hall, John Breden Sr, Golder Davison, George Rogers Jr, Joseph Johnson, Henry McGuffey Sr, William Barton are appointed as a Grand Jury.
-Willis vs Nathaniel Smith
-Gabriel Penn is appointed to take care of the Courthouse and keep same in order.
-On the motion of Edward Lewis, invalid pensioner, to be paid 15pounds out of the 1793 collection.
-Edward Lewis appeared in Court touching his inability as a pensioner
-John Turner a Commission appointing him Ensign of Militia
-On the motion of James Stewart Gentleman of the Law, leave is granted him to practice Law in this Court.
-Sumpter vs Reaves
-Blankenship vs Chitwood
-Deed- George Maberry Sr and George Maberry Jr to David Morgan further proved.
-Deed- Benjamin Butterworth to William Burnett
-Deed- Edward Brammer to Hugh Boyd
-Dean vs Smith
-Allen vs Shelton
-Deed- Joshua Hudson to Robert Hall
-Deed- Joshua Hudson to Golder Davison

PAGE 90

COURT Friday 27 February 1795 present, Archelaus Hughes, James Lyon, Francis Turner, Charles Foster, John Breden Jr, Hamon Critz Jr.
-Power of attorney of Elisabeth Sisom to William Keaton
-Hudspeth vs Ogle
-Hart Campbell & Co vs Call
-Gilbreath vs Breden Sr
-Deed- Hugh Armstrong to John Walter
-Sheriff to pay Charles Vest 30 pounds out of the 1793 fees in addition to the price of building the Courthouse, the difference between an outside chimney and an inside one as ascertained by Samuel Shelton.
-Breden Jr and wife vs Ruble and wife, referred to Joshua Rentfro, Joseph Lewis, Peter Young, George Penn, David Barton, Swinfield Hill, Samuel Staples, Stephen Smith, Thomas Goodson Sr, Francis Turner, Thomas Goodson Jr and Hugh Martin.
-Penn vs Tuggle

Page 90 contd

-Administration of the estate of Bartholomew Foley dec'd is granted Barberry Foley the widow who qualified according to Law with David Morgan, John Ferrell, Elisabeth Deweese, Mary Foley, Rachel Foley, Barberry Foley, Nelly Folley and Betty Foley her securities.
-Ordered that the order of September Court last for the division of the estate of B. Foley and for alloting the widow her third be rescinded.
-John Branham alias Parmer came into Court with William James Mayo, William Gardner his security. John Branham alias Parmer bond Fifty pounds to be of good behavior towards Moses Reynolds 1 month 1 day.
-William Branham alias Parmer came into Court with David Morgan as his security, furnished bond, to be of good behavior towards Moses Reynolds.
-Rowan vs Clark
-Hairston vs Cornwell

PAGE 91

-On the motion of Joseph Keaton judgement is granted him against William Mankin in the amount of £6.8.4, 8.62 and cost for paying so much to William Adams for security for the said William Mankin.
-Moore vs Mankin, Joseph Keaton Special Bail
-Moore vs William Willis and Joel Willis
-Perkins Sr vs Mayberry Jr
-Anderson & Co assignee of Henry Lyne vs George Mayberry Sr and Jr.
-Garrison vs McPeak
-Ogle vs Walter
-James Boyd 2 days witness John Ogle vs John Walter
-Isaac Dodson 2 days witness James Lyon vs N. Smith
-Deed- Benjamin Butterworth to William Burnett
-Salisbery vs Gee
-William Salsbery allowed 2 days this Court and 2 days last Court for Richard Salisberry vs Gee
-McCrery & Wallace vs Griffin on an atta. Rodham Moore saith he owes nothing.
-Stovall vs Keaton
-Gilliam vs Mullins on an atta. Abraham Eads a garnishee being sworn saith he owes Defendant nothing.
-Deed- William James Mayo to Valentine Mayo
-Corn vs Smith, deposition of Nancy Tindal to be taken
-Henry Smith allowed 1 day witness James Lyon vs Henry Smith
-Leander Hughes recommended as Deputy Surveyor for the County, to undergo examination by Henry County surveyor.

PAGE 92

COURT Saturday 18 February 1795 present: Samuel Clark, James Lyon, Abraham Penn, Archelaus Hughes, John Breden Jr
-Power of attorney of James Lyon to John Pace
-Hughes vs Frans referred to George Taylor and Balinger Wade
-Peter Scales 2 days witness Terry Hughes vs William Frans
-Abijah Hughes allowed 2 days 28 miles for same

County Levy for 1794 brought forward	79.17
Edward Tatum for Garrett Gibson, 5 young wolf heads	10.45
S. Staples for William Deal,Jr, 6 " " "	12.50
Joseph Bartlett, 1 old wolf head in 1790	2.8
To the Clerk	50.
To depositum for use of County	300.
Sheriff for collecting 1023 tithes	27.30
	481.50
By 1023 tithes at 47¢ per poll	481.50

-Rowan vs Baker
-Saunders vs Frazier
-Ordered that the Sheriff pay Abraham Penn £90.15 out of the depositum in his hands for the years 1792,1793 a balance due him for building the Prison, pillory and stocks after said stocks are delivered.

Page 92 contd

-John Fletcher 2 days witness James McCain vs Harvey Fitzgerald
-Munford Smith same
-Isbell vs Smith
-Ordered that instead of the first Monday in April next the Sheriff advertise that on the 2nd Monday the election of the Overseers of the Poor will be held.
-Smith vs Poteet Jr, jury sworn:Peter Scales, John Fletcher, William Sublett, George Fulcher, Munford Smith, John Clark, Joseph Reynolds, Noah Parr, Gabriel Penn, William France, John Mankin and Abraham Eads.
-John Poteet 4 days witness James Poteet Jr vs Humphrey Smith
-Kimzey vs Gee
-Penn vs Carlin
-Thomas Jett 2 days 35 miles witness Noah Parr vs Samuel Staples

PAGE 93

-Willis vs B. Smith
-McCain vs Fitzgerald
-Saunders vs Perry
-Ordered the Sheriff pay Charles Vest L80. out of the depositum in his hands for the years 1792,1793 in part for the building of this Courthouse.
-Deed- James Lyon to Henry Koger
-Ordered that the prison fees amounting to L37.6 for maintaining Robert Taylor ads Williamson & Garland in the Bill of Costs.
-Staples vs Parr, jury sworn: Elisha Harbour, Hobart Smith, John Poteet, Joseph Reynolds, John Mankin, Humphrey Smith, Jarrett Hums?, John Norton, William Sublett, William Adams, William J. Mayo, Valentine Mayo. Verdict for Defendant, appealed.
-Gabriel Penn 5 days witness George Baker vs Robert Rowan
-Samuel Staples 2 days for same
-Edward Tatum 1 day for same
COURT Thursday 27 March 1795 present: Archelaus Hughes, Jonathan Hanby, William Banks, Gabriel Penn, Charles Thomas
-Deed- Thomas Garrison to John Tuggle
-Deed- William Ison to Jonathan Ison
-Last Will and Testament of Frederick Fulkerson dec'd exhibited by Milley Fulkerson widow and relict
-Deed- James Taylor to John Medley Jr
-Deed- James Taylor to John Adams
-Deed- James Slater to Henry Koger
-Deed- William Stone to William Nowlin
-Deed- Edward Oneal to John Benian
-Henry McGuffery is exempt from payment of levies for the future.
-Deed- William Pilson to John Turner
-Deed- James Shelton and wife Susannah to Samuel Staples
-Deed- James Lyon to Gabriel Penn
-Lindsay & Hughes vs Shelton
-Becknall vs Allen and Bailey

PAGE 94

March Court: Archelaus Hughes, Jonathan Hanby, Stephen Lyon, Charles Thomas, James Lyon, William Banks, Brett Stovall, John Breden Jr, William Carter, Munford Smith, Joseph Stovall.
-Samuel Packwood is recommended as a Commissioner of the Peace.
-John Jones is appointed surveyor of the road from Collin Hamptons to the top of the Good Spur of the Blue Ridge.
-Gibson vs Hooker
-On the motion of Charles Vest by his attorney, a judgement is granted him against Daniel Carlin, Sheriff of this County for L80. and cost.
-Adkinson vs Boyd
-Dewitt vs Douglas
-Carlin vs Boyd
-Pennington vs Bristoe
-Cole vs Rowark
-Dugan vs Killey
-J. Gibson vs Polson
-Dewitt vs Hall
-Baker vs Griffin
-Lewis vs Perkins Sr

Page 94 contd

-Branham vs Helton
-Call vs Steel
-Martha Fontaine is administratrix of E. Henry dec'd vs John Hammonds Jr..dismissed
-Adkinson vs Bo....
-Hairston vs Stratton
-Commonwealth vs Fitzgerald
-Shelton vs Jones
-Reynolds vs Blackly
-Hall vs Spray
-Shelton vs Mankin
-Armstrong vs Codey
-Brooks vs Lawson
-Deed- William Banks to Hamon Frans
-Deed- John Barrett to Munford Smith
-Lewis vs Perkins Sr referred to Samuel Hairston and Peter Saunders
-Deed- Hamon Critz Jr to Samuel Clark Jr
-Deed- Edward Tatum to John Tatum and Jesse Tatum
-Deed- Brett Stovall to Wilson Penn and Gabriel Penn Jr
-Staples vs Griffin
-Samuel King for B. Of P. Saunders
-------- vs Adams Jr
-Irvine White & Co vs Hays
-McCrery & Co vs Bailey
-Redman vs Smith
-Lyon vs Adams, Samuel Packwood a garnishee being issued saith he owes the Defendant 16.19.4.

PAGE 95

-Power of attorney of James Lyon to James Taylor
-Baker vs Rowan
-Elijah Banks qualified as Ensign of the Militia
COURT 30 April 1795 present: Charles Foster, Gabriel Penn, Joseph Stovall, Abraham Penn
-Deed- John Hord and Stanwix Hord to John Redd
-Deed- Thomas Oldham to James Ferrell
-Deed- Robert Hughes to Lucy Barnard
-Deed- John Lee Sr to John Lee Jr
-Deed- John Parr Jr to Noah Parr
-Deed- Joseph Reynolds to James Turner
-Margaret Ferrell wife of James Ferrell relinquishes her right of dower to a deed of 360 acres conveyed to Nance Perdue.
-Deed- John Lee Sr to Edmund Brammer
-Deed- George Penn to George Fulcher
-Deed- Margaret Bristoe to Richard Massey
-Deed-Anthony Street to Edward Lewis
-Deed- Samuel Croucher Sr to Charles Croucher
-Deed- Nathaniel Ross to David Ross
-Deed- Charles Thomas to Robert Pennington
-Deed- John Watson Sr to William Heath
-Deed- Daniel Carlin to James Carlin
-Deed- John Cavin to Abraham Mayse
-Deed- Thomas Posey to Harrison Hubbert
-Deed- Harrison Hubbert to John Dillion
-Deed- William Read to Simon Dodson
-Deed- George Yeats to Henry Fry
-Deed- Gabriel Penn to Isaac Dodson
-Deed- Gabriel Penn to Thomas Bolling and Robert Sharp
-Deed- David Lawson to Joseph Garrett

PAGE 96

-Deed- William Smith Jr to William Smith Jr, Henry Smith and Nathaniel Smith
-Deed- Daniel Barnard and wife Mary to Palmer Critchfield
-Deed- Isham Webb to William Webb
-A lease of term of years from Jesse Corn to James Poteet and John Poteet
-Deed- Daniel Barnard and wife Mary to John Walter
-Deed- Morning Webb, Isuin? Webb and wife, Mary Quillin, Martin Deal

Page 96 contd

and wife to John Jones
-Deed- David Harbour to Martin Amos
-Deed- Edmund Brammer to Hugh Boyd
-Deed- Samuel Hooker to William Hooker
-Deed- Jesse Dodson to James Purdy
-Deed- John Gray to John Rust
-Deed- Bartlett Reynolds to John Gray
-Deed- Abram Penn to John Chitwood
-Deed- Abram Penn to Benjamin Philpott
-Deed- Abram Penn to Daniel Slater
-Deed- Abram Penn to John Newman Jr
-Deed- Abram Penn to Edmund Chitwood
-Deed- Abram Penn to Robert Sharp
-Deed- William Burress to John Burress
-Susannah Reynolds wife of Moses Reynolds relinquishes her right of dower to 339 acres conveyed by her husband to Samuel Croucher
-Deed- Isham Burnett to Samuel Henry
-Deed- John Pulliam and John Randals to Adrian Anglin
-Hairston vs Rickman, John Clark Spl Bl
-Deed- William Banks to John Frans Jr
-Deed- William Banks to Patrick Coleman
On the motion of Nathaniel W. Dandridge Jr leave is granted him to practice Law in this Court
-Deed- William Donathan to Peter Bowman
-Deed- William Green to Joseph Pratt
-Deed- Richard Adams to Jacob Critz
-Power of attorney from James Armstrong to Munford Smith

PAGE 97

-Deed- Thomas Hill to Jacob Critz
-Deed- James Slater to Henry Koger
-Tatum vs Pulliam
COURT Friday 1 May 1795 present: A. Hughes, Abram Penn, Charles Foster, Brett Stovall, Gabriel Penn, William Banks
-On a motion of Ann Banks the Trustees formerly appointed to take possession of her deceased husband James Banks estate, they refused to act, and it is ordered that Adam Banks be appointed.
-William Lindsay appointed Deputy Sheriff
-William Preston Skillern appointed Deputy States Attorney for this County.
-William Banks, James Taylor and James Lyon are appointed overseers of the Lower District, south of Bull Mountain, the superintendent having failed to attend the Election.
-William Banks, James Lyon qualified as Overseer of the Poor
-Salsberry vs Gee
-Perse Gruin is exempt from the payment of levies for the future
-Hairston vs Rickman, John Clark, Spl Bl
-Banks vs Breden Jr
Ordered the Overseer of the Poor bind out Shadrick Smith illigemate child; Elizabeth Barrett, Lucynda Barrett, Dicy Barrett, Jesse Helton, Margaret Helton.
-Hairston vs Francis, James Dickerson Spl Bl
-Hughes vs Hairston
-Perkins Sr vs Maberry Jr, referred to Samuel Hairston, John Poteet son of James Poteet, John Hall and David Morgan or any three.
-Penn vs Pulliam, Gabriel Penn saith he owes Defendant
-Crouch vs Pulliam

PAGE 98

-Shelton vs Allen, referred to George Penn and Stephen Lyon
-Commonwealth vs Mayberry
-Bone vs Joseph Adkinson
-Commonwealth vs Mayberry Jr
-William Peak 2 days witness Commonwealth vs Mayberry

Page 98 contd

-Dean vs Smith referred to A. Hughes, James Young, John Dethridge, Augustine Thomas, Joseph Taylor and Stephen Lyon or any three.
-Frans vs Going, referred to James Lyon and William Carter
-Massey vs Austin, defendant to take deposition of Charles Thomas, Jo. Perigo, Neimah Underwood, Nathan Hall, Edmond Brammer, Cary Hardwick.
-Alexander Lackey 2 days witness Commonwealth vs Mayberry
-Adam Turner same
-Soloman Stephens 3 days for same
-William Burnett 1 day for same
-Nathaniel N. Helton 3 days for same
-Charles Foster 2 days for same
-Richard Pilson Jr 2 days for same
-John Ferrell 2 days for same
-Joseph Breden 2 days for same
-Lyne vs Kimsey
-Commonwealth vs Guin
-Commonwealth vs Rowan
-George Carter and James Dickerson qualify as Overseers of the Poor.
-Smith vs Walden
-Hairston vs Cornwell
-Ogle vs Walden
-Blankenship vs Chitwood
-Kimzey vs Gee
-Penn vs Carlin
-Isbell vs Smith
-Fulcher vs Fulcher, Harvey Fitzgerald Special Bail. Jury sworn: Joseph Adkinson, Alexander Lackey, Munford Smith, Richard Adkinson, Amos Rowark, William Cornwell, Henry Smith, William Sowell, Jesse Reynolds, Harvey Fitzgerald, James Taylor, William McCrery..verdict for Pltf.

PAGE 99

April Court 1795
-Henry Smith 1 day witness James Lyon vs Smith
-John Norton 1 day 28 miles witness William Cornwell vs George Hairston
-Leave is granted Robert Rowan to retail spiritious liquors at his house in the Town of Taylorsville. Robert Scott his security.
-Reuben George 3 days witness Hubert Smith vs Isbell
COURT 2 May 1795 present: Abram Penn, Samuel Clark, Stephen Lyon and Gabriel Penn.
-On the motion of Daniel Carlin to stay a judgement obtained against him by Charles Vest, that £39.13.1 of said judgement be enjoined, his security Edward Tatum.
-Brown vs Rowan, dism
-Isbell vs Lawson
-Ecton vs Renn
-Baker vs Rowan
-Nowlin vs Critz
-Walter vs Hickenbottom
-Lyon vs Guilliam
-Baker vs Rowan, jury sworn: William Rogers, Elihu Ayrs, Gerrod Hume, Herbert Smith, William McCrery, Edmund Chitwood, William Rea, Patrick Fontaine, Jacob McCraw, Reuben George, Harvey Fitzgerald, Charles Vest..verdict for Pltf.. new tryall granted.
-Jacob Baker allowed 2 days witness George Baker vs Robert Rowan
-Charles Vest 2 days for same
-Gabriel Penn 2 days for same
-Samuel Staples 2 days for same
-Edward Tatum Esquire 2 days witness James Lyon vs N. Smith and 1 day Jos. Francis vs David Going.

PAGE 100

-James Lyon Jr recommended as Captain of a Company of Militia 2nd Btn
-Jacob McCraw 2 days witness Robert Rowan vs Augustine Brown
-John Williamson 4 days for same
COURT Thursday 28 May 1795 present: Archelaus Hughes, William Banks, Francis Turner and Charles Thomas.

Page 100 contd

-Perkins Sr vs Mayberry Jr
-Lewis vs Perkins Sr
-Redman vs Smith
-Overseers of the Poor bind out Sarah Gibson, Elisabeth Gibson, Jemimah Gibson and Mary Gibson.
-A certificate from Jonathan Hanby Gentleman Justice certifying that Edward Tatum took the oath as Commissioner for the County.
-Deed- Joseph Keaton to William Fitzgerald
-Deed- John Koger to George Hairston
-John Hall appointed surveyor of the road from Shooting Creek to Joint Crack Creek in place of Levy Perigo.
-George Corn appointed surveyor of the road from the ford of Spoon Creek above Hamon Critz to the....above Shadrick Barretts.
-Baker vs Rowan
-Francis Turner allowed 2 days witness William Perkins vs Mayberry also 1 day Commonwealth vs Mayberry
-Gibson vs Polson
-Carlin vs Boyd
-Rowan vs Baker
-Deed- George Hairston to Jesse Corn
-Pennington vs Bristoe
-Branham vs Helton
-Jacob Baker 1 day witness Baker vs Rowan
-Samuel Staples 1 day for same

Page 101

-Hairston vs Stratton
-Armstrong vs Cody
-Staples vs Griffin
-Fontaines attorney vs Garrison
-McAlexander vs Breden Jr
-Rowan vs Keaton
-Shelton vs Mankin
-Shelton vs Jones
-Irvine White & Co vs Hays
-Hairston vs Lackey
-Rowan vs Sharp
-Hairston vs Cornwell
-Francis vs Going
-King for the B. of Saunders vs McGee
-John Dillard 2 days 20 miles witness William Cornwell vs Geo. Hairston
-John Norton 1 day 28 miles for same
-Guinn vs Hayes
COURT Thursday 25 June 1795 present: Samuel Clark, Jonathan Hanby, James Lyon and Edward Tatum
-Deed of Gift- Frederick Fulkerson to James Fulkerson
-Deed- John Gee to Benjamin Morris
-Last Will and Testament of Frederick Fulkerson ordered recorded.
-Noah Parr appointed surveyor of the road from the South Mayo to Spoon Creek in place of George Corn
-Pennington vs Bristoe
-Branham vs John Helton
-Hairston vs Stratton

PAGE 102

-Shelton vs Mankin
-Armstrong vs Cody
-Rowan vs Sharp
-French vs Philpott
-Shelton vs Jones
-Staples vs Griffin
-Penn vs Helton
-Bolling vs Going
COURT Thursday 20 July 1795 present: William Banks, Samuel Clark, Francis Turner, Archelaus Hughes, Brett Stovall
-Deed- Joseph Griffin attorney in fact for William Griffin to Rhodah Moore, Barbary Griffin wife of Joseph, relinquishes dower right.
-Deed- Joseph Boyd to David McGowan
-Deed- William Halbert to William Smith
-Administration of the estate of Frederick Fulkerson dec'd granted to Milley Fulkerson,widow, relict and James Fulcher, security: A. Hughes Sr and Samuel Clark Sr.
-Peter Scales, William Gray, Jacob Critz, Isaac Adams or any three to appraise the estate.
-An instrument of writing from John Ellison relative to the

Page 102 contd

emancipation of a negro man slave, property of the said John Ellison was presented in Court and ordered recorded
-James Taylor foreman, Woody Burge, Benjamin Sanders, Samuel Kennon, Beveridge Hughes, William Lawson, Jesse Reynolds, George Penn Sr, James Thompson, George Rogers Jr, Anthony Collings, Robert Hall, John Crum, William Sharp, Jesse Corn, Henry Falkner, John Poteet and Obediah Hudson to serve as Grand Jury.
-Rowan vs France
-Samuel Clark Jr for the benefit of France

PAGE 103

-A. Banks vs Breden Jr, John Breden Sr, Spl Bl
-Rowan vs Breden Jr
-W. Ford vs Breden Jr, Andrew Breden Spl Bl
-G. Mayberry Jr vs Breden Jr
-William Armstrong vs Cody
-On the motion of James Boyd by attorney an injunction granted him to stay the Judgement obtained by James Carlin till heard in Equity
-Gilbreath assignee vs Breden Sr
-Lyne vs Tittle
-Deed of Trust - Hamon Frans to William Banks
-Jonathan Hanby, Samuel Clark and William Carter recommended as fit persons to serve as Sheriff.
-Staples vs Sheltons heirs

PAGE 104

COURT Friday 31 July 1795 present: Charles Foster, Edward Tatum, Francis Turner, Charles Thomas, Abraham Penn, Gabriel Penn
-Deed- Ezekiah Shelton to William Barton..Jane wife of Ezekiah Shelton relinquishes her dower to this property
-Garrison vs McPeak
-Dillion vs Hubbert, referred to Abraham Penn and John Dillard
--Ogle vs Walter Sr, Richard Adkinson Spl Bl, each party to take depo. of Mary Henderson for Pltf, Milley Boyd for Defd.
-James Boyd 4 days witness John Ogle vs John Walter
-Mary Henderson 4 days for same
-Benjamin Yeates 4 days for same
-Blankenship vs Chitwood
-Kimzey vs Gee
-Isbell vs Smith
-Reuben George 2 days witness Herbert Smith vs B. Isabell
-Mathew Moore 2 days for same
-Isbell vs Lawson
-Walter vs Hickinbottom
-Lyon vs Gilliam
-Collier vs Hammond
-Moore vs Douglas
-Baker vs Rowan..on a former order of Court.
-Clark vs Rowan, jury sworn: Samuel Clark, William Easley, Miller Easley, James Lyon Jr, Joel Chitwood, James Bailey, Jesse Corn, Robert Sharp, Roger Shelton, Joseph Reynolds, John Hammonds Jr and John Poteet. verdict for Pltf, new tryal granted Defd.
-Hairston vs Newman
-J. Penn vs Carlin

PAGE 105

-A list of taxable property from under the hand of Edward Tatum Commissioner of the County entered for the year 1795.
-Edward Tatum produced his account for services rendered and the Court allowed him $70.00.
-On a motion of William Cornwell by his attorney to stay proceedings of a judgement against him by George Hairston until same can be heard was over ruled by the Court.

Page 105 contd

-Frans vs Croucher, Henry Lyne Special Bail
-Smith vs Corn, jury sworn: Gabriel Penn, John Fletcher, Herbert Smith, David Rogers, James Bailey, George Rogers, Golder Davison, Thomas Bolling, Nathaniel Ross, Jesse Reynolds, John Medley, John Adams. verdict for Defendant
-Deed- Edward Tatum to John Tatum and Jesse Tatum
-Griffin vs McCrery & Wallace
-Brooks vs Lawson
-McCrery and Wallace vs Griffin
-Griffin vs Ross
-Rowan vs Pulliam, jury sworn: Gabriel Penn, Herbert Smith, Nathaniel Ross, Samuel Dalton, Jesse Reynolds, Moses Reynolds, Samuel Crutcher, Nathan Smith, James Bailey, William Fletcher, John Fletcher, John Hall,..verdict for Pltf
--Ezekiel McPeak 2 days witness H. Smith vs Corn
-Ordered that the Jailor have the prison door checked and repaired
County Levy for the year 1795
Clerks Salary $25.00; Sheriff 25.,Deputy States Attorney $25.00.

PAGE 106

COURT 1 August 1795 present: Gabriel Penn, Archelaus Hughes, Edward Tatum, James Lyon, William Carter and Brett Stovall.
-Alexander Banks vs Breden Jr
-Vest vs Saunders
-Hall vs Lawson
-Lawson vs William Bolling
-Lawson vs Edward Hall
-Hall vs Jones
-Going vs Rowan
-Nowlin vs Nowlin
-Frans vs Croucher
-Smith vs Shelton
-Lyon vs Bailey
-Hairston vs Francis
-Hughes vs Hairston
-Rowark vs Bone
-William Adams 3 days witness Robert Hall vs Jacob Lawson
-Golder Davison 3 days for same
-Sally Davison 3 days for same
-Shelton vs Jones
-Lyon vs Smith

PAGE 107

COURT Thursday 27 August 1795 present: Charles Foster, Edward Tatum, Samuel Clark, Gabriel Penn, Archelaus Hughes, Charles Thomas.
-Deed- William Stone to William Nowlin
-Deed- Charles Collier to John Smallman
-Golder Davison is appointed surveyor of the road from the forks below Edward Tatum to the forks below David Hanby in place of David Hanby.
-Deed- Hamon Frans to Henry Frans
-Deed of Trust- Hamon Frans to William Banks
-An inventory of the estate of Frederick Fulkerson returned
-The Overseers of the Poor to bind out James Rickman and Charles Rickman orphans.
-A release of a certain tract of land convyed formerly from William Branham Sr to John Frans in Trust.
-Jesse Reynolds is appointed surveyor of the road from the banks of the Mayo at the mouth of Penns lane to James Taylors in place of John Cameron.
-David Harbour appointed surveyor of the road from the top of Bull Mtn from Corns old place to the Widow Foleys.
-Pennington vs Bristoe
-Branham vs Helton
-Josiah Farris is appointed Captain of the Militia in place of Samuel Crutcher who hath resigned. Charles Crutcher appointed Lieutenant and Gabriel Penn appointed Ensign.
-John Tatum appointed Lt; George Rogers Jr appointed Ensign.
-Smith vs Shelton, James Lyon security for costs
-Hairston vs Stratton
-Hairston vs J. Pulliam
-Staples vs Griffin

PAGE 108

COURT Friday 28 August 1795 present: James Lyon, Abram Penn, Edward Tatum, William Carter, Archelaus Hughes, Samuel Clark

County Levy brought forward	75.
Bartlett Smith, 1 young wolf head	2.8
Samuel Staples for John Christian same	2.8
Samuel Staples for service to Commissioner	40.
Depositum for use of county	160.
By Claim of Deputy States Attorney, wrong levy	25.
Sheriff .06cents for collecting 254	15.24
	269.40
By 972 tithes @ .27 per poll	262.44
	6.96

-Thomas Whitlock, Martin Dickerson and Joseph R. Johnson are appointed to procession all the lands within the bounds of the Whitlock Company of Militia.
-William Carter, William Guin, Rhoda Moore same within the district of Munford Smiths Company.
-Jacob Critz, Augustine Thomas, Samuel Clark Jr the same in Critz District.
-James Taylor, George Penn Sr and William Willis same in Josiah Farris Company
-Charles Thomas, William Fuson, Barnard M. Price same in John Poteets Company
-William James Mayo, David Morgan, James Turner same in Jesse Corns Company.
-French vs Philpott
-Joshua Adams appointed surveyor of the road from the Bull Mountain to the Patrick Courthouse in place of Harvey Fitzgerald.
-Sheriff to pay Charles Vest 34 pounds 15 shillings.
-Ordered that James Lyon and Edward Tatum, gentlemen, be appointed Commissioners to let to the lowest bidder the repairs to the prison.
-Shelton vs Mankin
-Penn vs Going
-Bolling vs Going
-Tatum vs Dewit
-Tatum vs Manning
-Coroner to summon Daniel Carlin.

PAGE 109

COURT Thursday 24 September 1795 present: Samuel Clark, Francis Turner, Archelaus Hughes, William Banks
-Deed- Barberry Foley and others to Elisabeth Laurence
-Deed- Henry Frans to Peter Frans
-Augustine Thomas, Absolum Scales, Peter Frans, Samuel Clark Jr or any three to view the ford of the Spoon Creek near the Meeting House and report whether the ford can be made passable without a bridge.
-David Keaton appointed surveyor of the road from the South Mayo to Spoon Creek in place of Noah Parr
-Deed- John Gee to Benjamin Morris
-On a motion of William Banks, gentleman, Collector of the subscription for opening the navigation of the Dan River vs John Frans and John Fletcher.
-Deed- James Shelton and wife Susannah Shelton to William Hamblit
-Power of attorney of Eliphaz Shelton to Thomas Mitchell
-Smith vs Shelton, Pltf to take depo of George Elenon??
-George Penn, Edward Tatum, Joseph Stovall or any two to settle with the Overseers of the Poor and report.
-David Morgan, James Turner, John Tuggle, James Denny or any three to view a way for a road from the upper end of the said David Morgans plantation to Francis Turners.
-Deah Hudson is appointed surveyor of the road from the ford of Little Dan River to Peters Creek in Hanbys lande in place of Joseph Francis.
-Branham vs Helton
-Sheriff to pay James Taylor 17/6 for repairs to the Jail

Page 109 contd

-Rowan vs Sharp
-Shelton vs Mankin
-Ezekiah Shelton vs Going

PAGE 110

-Daniel Carlin appeared in Court with James Lyon, William Carter, Robert Rowan, Jonathan Hanby, Edward Tatum as his security for the collecting of revenue of 1794.
-Tatum vs Dewitt
-Fontaine vs Clark
-Salsberry vs Ferrell
-Crowder for the benefit of Dunkley vs Scales
-Callaway vs Miller
-Going vs Going
-Hume vs Hanby
-Lyon vs Going
-Lyon vs Fitzgerald
-Penn vs Going
-McPeak vs Kimzey
-William Banks is allowed 1 day as witness Gerard Hume vs Jonathan Hanby.
-Anderson & Co vs Maberry Jr
-Saunders vs Gardner
-Jesse Tatum is recommended as Lieutenat; William Adams as Ensign to the Samuel Staples Company.
COURT 29 October 1795 present: William Banks, Archelaus Hughes, Francis Turner, Samuel Clark, James Lyon, Edward Tatum.
-Corn vs Bolt
-Deed- Thomas Morrow executor of John Small deceased to James Denny
-Deed- Samuel Shleton to James Innes
-Deed- Jacob Critz to John Miller
-Smith vs Lackey
-Deed- Jonathan Cummings to Samuel Bower Hawkins
-Jury sworn: James Taylor foreman, William Keaton, Richard Davidson, Golder Davison, Moses Harbour, Moses Reynolds, George Rogers Sr, Joel Willis, James Bartlett, Richard Massey, Nathaniel N. Helton, Miller W. Easley, John Miller, Jesse Corn, Clement Rogers, Charles Rakes and Stephen Jones.

PAGE 111

-Corn vs Oldham
-Corn vs Maberry Jr
-Turner vs Read
-Keaton for the benefit of Adams Jr vs Frans
-Frans vs Crutcher
-Taylor vs Fletcher
-Saunders vs Price
-Thomas Mitchell came into Court with four lists of insolvents, two of which are for 1792, 1793 also two insolvents of property for the years 1792 and 1793.
-Jonathan Hanby produced a Commission appointing him Sheriff with bondsmen: A. Hughes Jr, Samuel Staples, Thomas Mitchell, David Rogers, Robert Rowan, John Walters, Barthlemew Smith, George Carter, William Carter, William Banks and James Lyon
-Deed- William Hickenbottom to John Walters
-Jonathan Hanby came into Court and offered to qualify as Sheriff agreeable to his Commission. Whereas the Court were of the opinion that he ought to not qualify untill the full expiration of the former sheriff.
-Walter vs Boyd

Court Adjourned

PAGE 112

COURT Tuesday 30 October 1795 present: James Lyon, Francis Turner, Charles Thomas, Joseph Stovall
-Deed- Cornelius Keaton to Nathan Stewart - 2 deeds
-On the motion of Henry Koger leave is granted him to keep an Ordinary at his home in the town of Taylorsville
-Hairston vs Newman
-Kimzey vs Gee
-Walter vs Hickenbottom
-Lyon vs Going
-Ogle vs Walters, jury sworn: William Moore, Thomas Hornsby, Thomas R. Hall, James Lyon, Nathaniel N. Helton, James Turner, David Rogers, Thomas Willis, David McGowin, Nathan Hall, James Boyd, Bethney Haynes
-Moore vs Carlin
-Lyon vs Gilliam
-James Boyd 2 days witness John Ogle vs John Walter
-Robert Hudspeth 2 days for same
-Mary Henderson 2 days for same
-John Ogle Jr 2 days for same
-Benjamin Yeats 2 days for same
-Milley Boyd 2 days for same
-McCrery & Wallace vs Griffin
-Penn vs Carlin, jury sworn: Thomas Hornsby, Thomas Hoff, James Lyon, Nathaniel N. Helton, David Rogers, Thomas Willis, Nathan Hall, James Boyd, William Fitzgerald, George Carter, Joseph Davis, William Moore. ..verdict for Pltf.
-McCrery & Wallace vs Griffin, jury sworn: John Walters, William Willis, Robert Sharp, George Rogers Jr, George Corn, Charles Rakes, Richard Massey, James Bailey, David Rogers, George Carter, Henry Fitzgerald, Stephen Jones..verdict for Pltf.
-Hall vs Lawson
-Austin vs Massey

PAGE 113

October Court 1795 present: James Lyon, Jonathan Hanby, William Carter, Stephen Lyon, Charles Thomas, Edward Tatum, Hamon Critz, Joseph Stovall, Munford Smith.
-Joshua Rentfro is recommended as a fit person to serve as a Commissioner of the Peace
-Edward Tatum is recommended as Commissioner
-Hall vs Jones, jury sworn: Joshua Rentfro, George Carter, James Bailey, Henry Smith, George Corn, Nathan Hall, John Fletcher, David Hanby, David Rogers, Samuel Harris, George Mayberry, James Taylor. Verdict returned for Pltf.
-Eliphaz Shelton 1 day witness Jones vs Robert Hall
-William Adams 3 days for same
-Elisabeth Shelton 2 days for same

PAGE 114

COURT continued for October 1795 Saturday the 31 st, present: Abram Penn, Edward Tatum, James Lyon, A. Hughes, Charles Thomas.
-Helton vs Rowan, Eliphaz Shelton, Spl Bl
-Garrett vs Lawson and wife
-On a motion of John Walter by his attorney an injunction is granted him to stay a Judgement obtained by John Ogle..David McGowan his security.
-Baker vs Rowan
-Clark vs Rowan
-Smith vs Shelton
-Hairston vs Francis
-Bailey vs Lyon
-Rowark vs Bone
-Nowlin vs Nowlin
-Lyon vs Bailey
-Hughes vs Francis

Page 114 contd

-Vest vs Saunders and others..jury sworn: Nathan Hall, Samuel Clark, Joseph Newman, Richard Adkinson, William Moore, David Rogers, James Taylor, George Rogers Jr, Jacob Lawson, Joseph Keaton, Robert Sharp, William Willis..verdict for Pltf.
-Nathan Hall 2 days witness George Baker vs R. Rowan
-Samuel Staples 2 days for same
-Richard Adkinson 3 days witness McCrery & Wallace vs Griffin
-Richard Adkinson 4 days for William Griffin vs McCrery & Wallace
-Breden Jr vs Maberry Jr
-Joseph Breden vs Mayberry Jr
-Baker vs Rowan, jury sworn: William Keaton, Joseph Newman, Frederick Fitzgerald, Terry Hughes, Samuel Clark,David Rogers, William Willis, Robert Sharp, John Hall, Thomas Willis, Adrian Anglin, Golder Davidson. Verdict returned for the Pltf.

PAGE 115

-Joseph Keaton 2 days witness Robert Hall vs J. Lawson
-George Rogers Jr 3 days for James Bailey vs James Lyon
-Tatum vs Pennington
-George Carter, Jonathan Hanby, Edward Tatum are appointed to let to the lowest bidder repairs to the Jail.
-David Rogers 3 days witness James Bailey vs Lyon
-William Willis 2 days for Joseph Breden vs G. Mayberry

COURT Thursday 26 November 1795 present: Samuel Clark, Hamon Critz, Stephen Lyon, Brett Stovall
-Deed- James Lackey to James Turner
-Deed of Gift- James Taylor to James Cummings
-Jonathan Hanby appeared in Court and produced a Commission appointing him Sheriff of the County.
-Daniel Carlin qualified as Justice of the Peace, Justice in Chancery, a Justice of Oyer andTerming.
-Hairston & Hughes vs Lyon and wife
-Deed- Elisabeth Sisam and Rubin Sisam to Robert Rowan and Robert Scott
-David Hanby Jr and Archelaus Hughes Jr qualified as Deputy Sheriffs
-Susannah Clark wife of John Clark relinquishes her right of dower to land conveyed by her husband to Richard Thomas.

PAGE 116

-Isaac Dodson allowed 1 day witness J. Lyon vs Nathaniel Smith
-William James Mayo appointed surveyor of the road from the top of Bull Mountain to Francis Turners in place of Thomas Morrow.
-Branham vs Helton
-Last Will and Testament of Hamon Critz deceased, exhibited.
-Shelton vs Going
-Tatum vs Dewitt
-Fontaines administrators vs Clark
-Peter Crowder for the benefit of Moses Dunkley vs Scales
-Going vs Goings Administrator
-Tatum vs Lackey and Sharp
-John Tatum qualified to collect his old assearers under Jonathan Hanby, Sheriff
-Hume vs Hanby
-Lyon vs Fitzgerald
-Rowan & Scott vs Breden
-Richard Adkinson vs Douglas
-Landreth vs Lawson
-Carter vs Hooker
-Koger vs Stewart
-Smith vs Shelton..Pltf to take depo of John Pulliam..Walker Baliles, John James, William Miller, John Turpin and William Bledsoe, Gentlemen, appointed to act as Commissioners to take said deposition or any 3.
-Carlin vs Mitchell

Page 116 contd

-On a motion of Humphrey Smith by his attorney request a stay of the proceedings of a Judgement brought by Richard Vest.

PAGE 117

COURT Monday 7 December 1795 present: James Lyon, Francis Turner, Samuel Clark, Hamon Critz
-On the examination of James Treasey on suspicion of feloniously breaking open a loom house of Pierce Guinn and carrying of a piece of liennor (linen?) and harness, defendant pleads not guilty. Court after consideration renders verdict of Not Guilty.

PAGE 118

COURT Thursday 31 December 1795 present: Abraham Penn, James Lyon, Francis Turner, Brett Stovall
-Deed- John Parr Sr to Clifton Keaton
-Deed- John Pulliam to John Randals
-Deed- Ann Walden to Edward Lewis
-William Green, Robert Green, William Carter and Rhoda Moore or any three of them to view a way for a road from Willis Cheeks to cross the mountain at Bells Spur and from thence to the County line, meeting a road from Grayson County and report.
-Deed- William Wells and John Clark to Richard Thomas
-On a motion of Theopelous Lacy who produced a license to practice Law in this County and other Courts.
-Deed- Archelaus Hughes Sr to Archelaus Hughes Jr
-Deed- William Willis to Joel Willis
-Abraham Hawks is appointed surveyor of the road from the Carolina line to the top of the mountain at Flower Gap.
-Henry Koger appointed surveyor of the road from John Camerons into the Bull Mtn. Rd.
-Deed- Anthony Collins to Ralph Danger
-Deed- John Chandler to Richard Adkinson - 2 deeds
-Report of a view of a road from Francis Turners to David Morgans.
-Ordered that David Roberson be appointed surveyor of the road above mentioned and Roberson to call on Henry Tuggle and his gang.
-Carlin vs Mitchell
-Thomas Bolling allowed 9 days as guard over the Jail.
-Gabriel Penn allowed 9 days for finding Treasey

PAGE 119

-Eliphaz Shelton is allowed 9 days for each of his sons for guarding the Jail over James Treasey.
-Jacob Adams allowed 2 days for the same.

COURT Friday 1 January 1796 present: Abraham Penn, Francis Turner, Hamon Critz, Brett Stovall
-Branham vs Helton
-Shelton vs Going
-Going Administrator vs Going
-Hume vs Hanby
-Lyon vs Fitzgerald
-Rowan vs Haile
-Rowan & Scott vs Breden
-Adkinson vs Douglas
-Tatum vs Hammon Sr
-Dickerson vs Boyd
-Ayres vs Boyd
-Yoes vs West
-John Tatum and John Dalton are recommended as Deputy Surveyors, to be examined by Humphrey Smith.

PAGE 120

COURT Thursday 28 January 1796 present: William Banks, Francis Turner, James Lyon, Samuel Clark.
-Deed- Benjamin Lewis to Hamon Critz
-Power of attorney of Abner Echols to William Fuson
-Deed- Jacob Adams Jr to Joseph Going - 2 deeds
-A report of the examination of John Dalton by Humphrey Smith touching his fitness for the office of Deputy Surveyor returned.

Page 120 contd

-John Dalton qualified under Senior Surveyor Brett Stovall.
-David Harbour is appointed Processioner in place of William Fuson.
-Deed- John Chandler to Richard Adkinson
Present: William Carter, Stephen Lyon, Edward Tatum, Brett Stovall, Hamon Critz. The Court is of the opinion that each Processioner do business seperately.
-Smith vs Fuson
-Dickerson vs Boyd
-Hughes vs ??
-Jonathan Hanby, Sheriff, objects to the insufficiency of the Jail.
Absent: William Carter, Stephen Lyon, Edward Tatum, Brett Stovall.
-John Burnett is appointed surveyor of the road from Charles Fosters to Coxs in place of Humphrey Smith.

-Laurence	vs Branham	-Branham	vs Helton
-Going	vs Going	-Hume	vs Hanby
-Lyon	vs Fitzgerald	-Rowan & Scott	vs Breden
-Adkinson	vs Douglas	-Rowan	vs Hale
-Yoes	vs West	-Dabney	vs Maberry

PAGE 121
COURT Thursday 25 February 1796 present: A. Hughes, James Lyon, Francis Turner, Charles Foster, Charles Thomas, George Penn.
-Deed- Thomas Hambleton to Henry Koger
-Deed- John Daniel to Richard Massey
-Deed- Robert Hall to Robert Sharp
-Deed- Thomas Harbour to Isham Craddock
-Commonwealth vs Roberson
- same vs John Hughes
- same vs Archelaus Hughes Jr
-Deal vs Going
-Deed- Henry McGuffey Sr to John P. Stegall, Letitia McGuffey wife of Henry McGuffey Sr relinquishes her right of dower
-Josiah Farris qualified as Captain of the Militia
-Rickman vs Posey
-Hanby vs Dunkin
-Deed- William Deal to Samuel Staples
-Grand Jury: James Taylor foreman, William Easley, Henry Smith, Humphrey Smith, John Miller, George Penn Sr, Moses Harbour, Humphrey Posey, Jesse Corn, Joel Willis, Augustine Thomas, Moses Reynolds, John France, Josias Farris, William Sharp and William Keaton.
-Saunders vs Price, George Lackey, Spl Bl
-Bryant vs Hall
-Dabney vs Maberry
-McAlexander vs Maberry
-Joshua Rentfro qualified as Justice of the Peace
-Tatum vs Going, William Carter, Spl Bl
-Commonwealth vs Stevens
- same vs Lawson
- same vs Mayo

PAGE 122

COURT Friday 26 February 1796 present: A. Hughes, Charles Foster, Francis Turner, William Banks, Gabriel Penn, Brett Stovall.
-Kimzey vs Jones jury sworn: Samuel Clark Jr, Robert Rowan, Charles Vest, Adam Turner, John Wallace, Robert Scott, John Dalton, William Lindsay, John Ogle, John Lackey, George Corn, Jacob Michaux..verdict returned for Pltf in the amount of one cent.

-Lyon	vs Gilliam	-Smith	vs Shelton
-Lyon	vs Bailey	-Hall	vs Lawson
-Bailey	vs Lyon	-Breden	vs Mayberry
-Breden Jr	vs Mayberry	-Pennington	vs Lawson
-Adkinson	vs Ross	-Helton	vs Rowan
-Baker	vs Rowan	-Smith	vs Shelton

-Garrett vs Lawson and wife, jury sworn: George Rogers, Gabriel Penn, Robert Sharp, James Lackey, Alexander Lackey, John Hanby, John Dalton, Roderick Shelton, Joseph Keaton, George Corn, Joel Chitwood, George

Page 122 contd
Penn Jr..

PAGE 123

-Hill & Co vs Chitwood
-Mayberry vs McAlexander
-Sutton vs Carlin
-Adams vs Keaton
-William Moore is appointed Captain of the Militia in place of Munford Smith who hath resigned
-William Smith is appointed Lieutenant, James L. Gains Ensign of the 2nd Battalian.
-Charles Foster is recommended as Captain of the Militia in place of John Poteet of the 1st Battalian.
-Munford Smith appointed Ensign in place of George Rogers who has removed, of the 1st Bttn.
-Gabriel Penn appointed Captain of Artillery; John Hughes as 1st Lt; William Lindsay as 2nd Lt..
-Samuel Duvall recommended as Deputy States Attorney in place of William P. Skillern.
-Adams Jr vs Going, referred to John Staples, Abraham Penn and William Shelton.
-McPeak vs Turner and Kimzey
-Alexander Lackey came into Court and returned an account of his proceedings as Officer of the Processioners, whereupon Andrew Breden, Richard Pilson and Alexander Lackey were allowed for 18 hours service.
-Alexander Lackey allowed 2 days for James Turner at the suit of William McPeak.
-Adam Turner 2 days for same

PAGE 124

COURT Saturday 27 February 1796 present: Archelaus Hughes, James Lyon, Stephen Lyon, Brett Stovall
-Edward Lewis an invalid pensioner, appeared in Court and his pension is to be continued.
-Samuel Clark vs Joseph Keaton, referred to Josiah Farris, William Banks and James Taylor.
-Webb vs Shelton
-Anderson and Co vs Banks
-Lyon vs Gilliam
-Smith vs Shelton, Pltf to take deposition of John Akin and Jacob Snail and wife..William Ship Hicks, Reuben George, John Sumpter and ---Vanderhose or any 3 to act as Commissioners.
-John Tatum qualified as Deputy Surveyor
-Deed- James McCain to James Dearman
-William Adams allowed 3 days witness Robert Hall vs Jacob Lawson
-Joseph Keaton 3 days for same
-Hughes vs France, award to defendant
-Adkinson vs Rowark
-Breden vs Breden..dismissed
-Donelson vs Deweese's executors
-Commonwealth vs Maberry for perjury, Court is of the opinion that the informer pay all costs.
-Robert Hall allowed 3 days witness Levey Smith vs Eliphaz Shelton
-Commonwealth vs Mabrary - nol pros
- same vs Michael Wardon
- same vs Doshia Wardon
- same vs Bow....
-Lawson vs Hall

PAGE 125

-James Lyon allowed 2 days witness Levey Smith vs Eliphaz Shelton and 1 day Benjamin Garrett vs Lawson and wife.
-William Adams presented a Commission appointing him Ensign of a Company of Riflemen.

Page 125 contd

-Gabriel Penn allowed 2 days Levy Smith vs E. Shelton
-Thomas Mitchell produced a voucher in the amount of depositium in his hands for the years 1791-1793 as Deputy Sheriff for William Mitchell and Daniel Carlin, Gentlemen Sheriffs.
COURT Thursday 31 March 1796 present: James Lyon, William Carter, Charles Foster, Edward Tatum, Charles Thomas
-Bill of Sale, John Sharp to Thomas Mitchell
-Deed- James Taylor to David Taylor
-Deed- Samuel Clark Jr to William Hanner
-Deed- Thomas Tennison to Humphrey Smith
-Power of attorney of Abner Echols to William Fuson further proved
-Deed- Dinah Critz and Elisabeth Critz to George Hairston
-John Rea appointed surveyor of the road from the ford of the Mayo near Frances old place to the Hollow Road near the Meadow Meetinghouse.
-Peter Scales appointed surveyor of the road from the ford of the Mayo near Frances old place to the Carolina line.
-Luaven Alley appointed surveyor of the road from A. Hughes to Fees Meadow
-Rowan vs Tuggle, dismissed
-Augustine Thomas one of the Processioners returned his list, allowed 6 days for service
-Jacob Critz same for 9 days
-Samuel Clark Jr same for 18 days
-James Taylor same for 23 days
-William Willis same for 28 days
-George Penn Sr same for 22 days

PAGE 126

-Deed- John Breden Sr and wife to Joseph Reynolds
-Charles Thomas allowed 20 days for processioning
-David Harbour 18 days for same
-William Fuson 4 days for same
-Thomas Whitlock 17 days for same
-Joseph Rea Johnson 12 days for same
-William James Mayo 53 days for same
-Jury do settle the dispute between Luke Foley and Jacob Saunders.
-James Turner allowed 9 days for processioning
-William Green 14 days for same
-Rhodah Moore 13 days for same
-Nathaniel Smith 25 days for same
-John Tatum 9 days for same
-James Lyon 14 days for same
-Thomas Whitlock qualified as Captain of the Militia
-Martin Dickerson as Lieutenant
-Hall vs Lawson, defendant to take deoposition of William Jones, William Bolling and Alexander Nelson..John Gordon, Thomas Jackson, William Payne and Stokley Donelson or any 3 to act as Commissioners.
-Hairston vs Adams Jr, dismissed
-On the motion of Jacob Adams Jr by his attorney to stay the proceedings of Edward Tatum vs Jacob Adams Jr.
-Ordered that the Surveyor and the Jury attend the land of John Burnett and Humphrey Smith.

PAGE 127

-Lawson vs Hall, Pltf to take depo of William Jones, William Bolling and Alexander Nelson. John Gordon, Thomas Jackson, William Payne and Stokley Donelson to act as Commissioners.
-Deed- Elisabeth Terry to William Carter
-J. Tatum vs Going, deposition of Martha Tatum to be taken.
-William Carter and Edward Tatum are appointed to view the repairs to the Jail.
-On a motion of John Douglas to stay a Judgement of Richard Adkinson, Tederick Yoes his security.
-David Morgan 1 day witness John Hughes vs J. Tuggle

Page 127 contd

-Yoes vs West, on a Judgement for six pounds, John Yeates alias Smith saith he owes Defendant three pounds in trade.

COURT Thursday 28 April 1796 present: A. Hughes, James Lyon, John Breden, Joshua Rentfro
-Deed- Abraham Penn to John Hill
-Deed- William McAlexander to Reuben Harris
-Deed- James Ingram to Fanny An Via
-Last Will and Testament of Fanny An Via returned and ordered recorded.
-Deed- William Austin to Jesse Corn
-Grand Jury for County: Peter Scales foreman, John Douglas, George Rogers, Joseph Garrett, William Garrett, Daniel Slater, Clement Rogers, Samuel Perry, William Sharp, John Turner, Barnard M. Price, Jeremiah Burnett Jr, James Bartlett, Micajah Burnett, Augustine Thomas, John Rea, William Sublett and Richard Miles.
-Barnard M. Price returned to Court his list of Processioning and was allowed 30 days for same.

PAGE 128

-Deed- Samuel Clark to Samuel Clark Jr
-Edward Tatum and William Carter viewed the Jail and the repairs done agreeable to contract.
-Deed- Daniel Newman and John Newman to Isaac Hollandsworth
-Deed- Richard Baker to Zachariah King
-Deed- Anthony Smith and wife to George Hairston
--Deed- Ignatious Redman and Hiller to George Hairston
-Deed- William Halbert to William Smith Sr
-Deed- Robert Sharp to William Lindsay and Jacob Michaux
-Deed- Dinah and Elisabeth Critz to George Hairston
-Deed- John Breden Sr to Joseph Reynolds

COURT Friday 29 April 1796 present: A. Hughes, James Lyon, Francis Turner, Munford Smith, Thomas Whitlock.
-Thomas Whitlock appeared in Court and qualified as Justice of the Peace
-Lyon vs Gilliam
-Bailey vs Lyon
-Lyon vs Bailey, jury sworn: Peter Saunders, Thomas Bolling, J. Hughes, William Walden, William Rogers, Isaac Dodson, Thomas Hornsby, Andrew Breden, William Webb, John Hall, Gabriel Penn, Joseph Breden..verdict for Pltf.
-Rentfro vs Perry
-Deed- Isham Webb and wife; John Jones and wife; Molleyan Haywood alias Quillin, Martin Doyle and wife to William Webb.
-Deed- Thomas Hambleton and wife Joyce Hambleton to Henry Koger
-Smith vs McCrery
-Hall vs Lawson
-Koger vs Hambleton

PAGE 129

-Joseph Breden by John his next friend vs G. Maberry Jr., jury sworn: Samuel Clark Jr, William Willis, Thomas Bolling, William Webb, William Rogers, Isaac Dodson, John Hall, Gabriel Penn, Thomas Hornsby, Jesse Tatum, David Rogers, George Fulcher..a juror withdrew,continued.
-Jesse Tatum Jr appointed Commissioner in place of Edward Tatum.
-Jesse Tatum Sr 2 days witness Stephen Lyon vs William Gilliam
-David Rogers 2 days for same
-Deed- Bartlett Reynolds to John Gray
-Rowan vs Brooks, John Tatum Spl Bl, defendant delivered into custody. William Cloud further Spl Bl
-Ordered the Sheriff to pay James Turner $15.50 for repairs to Jail.
-Breden Jr vs Maberry Jr
-Adkinson vs Joseph Ross

Page 129 contd

-Smith vs Shelton, the Defendant to take the deposition of Adam Snell, John Smith and Ro. Haile and William Heallty (Heatley?) Paul Worley, Thomas Sabb, John Dash and John Taylor or any three appointed Comissioners for this purpose and the the 13,14 or 15th of July next at William Heatleys.
-Morgan vs A. Breden..A. Hughes Spl Bl
-Tatum vs Going -- dismissed
-Pursuant to an Act of the Assembly, Courth doth set and rate the following Liquors, etc
Breakfast, if hot 1/3, otherwise 1/.
Dinner if hot 2/0, otherways 1/6
Lodging 4d, Corn 1/0 per gallon, oats 9d per gallon, sheaves oats 2d, bundle of fodder 1d
Rum if continental 16/0 per gallon
West Indian or Antiga 2/4 per gallon
Brandy, if good, 12/0 per gallon
Single distilled whiskey 10/,Double 12/,
Supper 1/6.

PAGE 130

COURT Saturday 30 April 1796 present: Francis Turner, Edward Tatum, Brett Stovall, Thomas Whitlock
-Garrett vs Lawson and wife
-McAlexander vs Maberry
-Sutton vs Carlin--dismissed
-Adams vs Keaton - contd
-Anderson & Co vs Banks..judgement
-Adkinson vs Rowark
-Donalson vs Smith, executor of Deweese
--Moore vs Carlin, jury sworn: Henry France Jr, William Lindsay, John Miller, Frederick Fitzgerald, John Mankin, Thomas Bolling, G. Penn, Malichiah Comings, Jesse Tatum, Henry Koger, Peter Dunavan, Robert Scott..verdict for Pltf.
-Bridgeman vs Bowman - dismd
-Ogle vs Boyd
-Bryant vs Hall
-Deed- Peter Dunavan to George Hairston
Present: Abraham Penn and William Carter.
-On a motion of Rowan & Scott leave is granted them to keep an Ordinary at their house in the town of Taylorsville with A. Hughes Jr their security.
-Deed- Daniel Carlin to John Tatum
-John Tatum, former Deputy Sheriff for Daniel Carlin Sheriff, returned 2 lists of insolvents for 1794, 1 for land and 1 for property.
-Deed- James Lyon to Robert Rowan and Robert Scott
-William Banks, Edward Tatum and Joshua Rentfro, Gentlemen, to view the Clerks and Surveyors office a make a report.
-Certificate from Brett Stovall, JP, relative to the qualifications of Jesse Tatum Jr as a Commissioner.
-Deed- James Lyon Sr attorney for Harris Wilson to Stephen Lyon
-Deed- Stephen Lyon to Matthew Moore
-James Lyon 2 days witness Benjamin Garrett vs D. Lawson
-Stephen Lyon 2 days for same

PAGE 131

-William Carter returned his proceedings as Processioner and was allowed 9 days.
COURT Thursday 26 May 1796 present: James Lyon, Stephen Lyon, Brett Stovall.
-Elley Lyon relinquishes her right of dower to deed issued William Moore
-Dged- John Botetourt to Samuel B. Hawkins
-Reynolds vs Medley, dismissed
-Inventory of the estate of Cornelius Deweese returned, also sales.

Page 131 contd

-Deed- Elisabeth Laurence to William Palmer Branham Jr
-John Parr with Jacob Critz hands and David Keatons hands to build a bridge across Spoon Creek at a place the former bridge was built.
-Keaton vs Going - dismd
-William Adams appointed surveyor of the road from the ford of Spoon Creek above Hamon Critz in place of George Corn
-Branham vs Helton, abates by death of Defendant
-Shelton vs Going..dismd
-Adrian Anglin 2 days witness Jesse Reynolds vs John Medley
-Laurence vs Branham Jr, judgement for Pltf
-Humphrey Smith 5 days witness Elisabeth Laurence vs William Branham
-Benjamin Hancock 3 days for same
-Henry McGuffey 3 days for same
-Joseph Reynolds 2 days for same
---- vs Hanby
-Clark vs Keaton, returned for Pltf
-Rowan vs Haile - judgement
-Rowan & Scott vs Tuggle - judgement
-Douglas vs Adkinson, Pltf to take deposition of William Scott
-William Howell appointed Constable in place of Am os Rowark
-Smith executor of Deweese vs Mankin
-Same vs Walden
-Sutherland vs Tuggle

PAGE 132

-Moore vs West
-A. Hughes vs McCain
-Hughes vs Tuggle
-Hairston vs Abbington
-Frans vs Scales
-Baker vs Rowan
-Sutton vs Tatum
-James Lyon Jr qualified as Captain of the Militia
-John Tatum qualified as Lieutenant
-John Tatum Jr as Lieutenant of a Rifle Company
-Keaton vs Hornsby
-Penn vs Carlin

COURT 30 June 1796 present: A. Hughes, Edward Tatum, Samuel Clark, Hamon Critz, William Banks, Joshua Rentfro
-Deed- George Tittle to Joseph Hale
-Deed- William Wells and John Clark to Richard Thomas
-Hume vs Hanby
-William Banks 1 day witness Gerald Hume vs Jonathan Hanby
-Aaron Rea exempt from payment of levies for the future.
-Zaphamiah Tenison appointed surveyor of the road from Charles Fosters to the Franklin line in place of Thomas Bristoe.
-Eliphaz Shelton 1 day witness Gerard Hume vs Hanby
-George Lackey appointed surveyor of the road from the top of Bull Mtn Rd to the Widow Foleys.
-Benjamin Hancock appointed surveyor of the road from the said Hancocks to the Bull Mtn Rd
-Smith, executor of Deweese vs Walden..dismissed
-Thomas Pusey 2 days witness William Walden vs H. Smith, executor of Deweese
-Featherstone Walden 1 day for same
-Sutherland vs Tuggle
-Saunders vs Henry
-Moore vs West

PAGE 133

-Hughes vs McCain
-Hairston vs Abbington
-Sutton vs Tatum

Page 133 contd

-Baker vs Rowan
-James Lyon, Samuel Staples, Benjamin Philpott and George Fulcher to view a road from Patrick Courthouse thru the said Staples plantation to said James Lyons.
-Smith vs Shelton, referred to John Dillard, Samuel Staples, Brett Stovall, Stephen Lyon and Joshua Rentfro
-Keaton vs Hornsby..dismd
-Adams vs Keaton
-Sumpter vs Bryant
-Hale vs Adams Jr
-Philpott vs Frans
-Eliphaz Shelton 1 day witness Joseph Keaton vs William Adams

COURT Thursday 28 July 1796 present: Francis Turner, Edward Tatum, Charles Thomas, Brett Stovall, Joshua Rentfro

-Adkinson vs Rowark
-Deed- George Tittle to Joseph Hale
-Deed- Aaron Walden to Edward Lewis
-Deed- Micajah Burnett to John Burnett..Sally Burnett wife of Micajah Burnett relinquished her right of dower
-Deed- Abraham Frazor to Christopher Long
-James Taylor foreman, Richard Mills, James Turner, Richard Pilson, Barnard M. Price, Nathaniel N. Helton, Joseph R. Johnson, Richard Davison, Isham Cradock, Richard Massey, William McAlexander, Edward Lewis, William Sharp, George Corn, John Tatum and James Denny sworn as Grandy Jury.
-John Tatum vs Adams..William Keaton Spl Bl
-Commonwealth vs Bowman
- same vs Cross

PAGE 134

-Smith vs Shelton..referees discharged and ordered to be redocketed
-Frost vs Taylor
COURT, A. Hughes, James Lyon, Stephen Lyon, Francis Turner, Edward Tatum, Joseph Stovall, Brett Stovall, John Breden, Joshua Rentfro, Hamon Critz, Charles Thomas.
-Jonathan Hanby, Samuel Clark and William Carter are recommended as proper persons to serve as Sheriff.

COURT 29 July 1796 present: A. Hughes, Francis Turner, Charles Thomas, Brett Stovall
-Lyon vs Gilliam
-Joseph Breden by his next friend John vs George Mayberry Jr, jury sworn: William McAlexander, Humphrey Posey, John Tuggle, William Roberson, Barnard M. Price, Robert Sharp, Jesse Tatum, Thomas Hall, George Corn, John Henry Jr, Elijah Dehart, Jeremiah Burnett Sr. verdict for Pltf
-Commings vs Webb - dismd
-Lyne vs Newman, Pltf agreed to stay proceedings to the 10th August next, then to be referred to George Penn and William Banks
--A receipt from George Hairston to Joseph Johnson for a Bond ordered recorded.
-Hall vs Lawson, jury sworn: Thomas Hornsby, David Rowark, James Lyon, Edward Lewis, John Miller, Joseph Reynolds, Henry Smith, Benjamin Hale, Samuel Clark, David Rogers, William Fitzgerald, Samuel Dalton. A juror withdrew and continued.
-Power of attorney of George Brooks to Jonathan Hanby
-Isaac Hollandsworth 4 days witness Joseph Breden by John his next friend vs G. Mayberry
-William Willis 5 days for same

PAGE 135

-Adkinson vs Ross, contd
-Gabriel Penn produced a Commission appointing him Captain of a

Page 135 contd

Company of Artillery
-William Lindsay, a Commission as 2nd Lt.
-Jesse Tatum, Gentleman, produced a list of taxable property for 1796.
-Howard vs Henslee - dismd
-John Hughes qualified as 1st Lt of Artillery
-Walter vs Ogle
-Deed- William Hickenbottom to Richard Adkinson
-Lyon vs Gilliam, jury sworn: John Turner, John Collins, William Sloan, Alexander Lackey, William McAlexander, Newman Helton, Nathaniel Ross, Joseph Keaton, Joel Willis, Reuben Harris, Henry Harris, Archibald Shelton..verdict for Pltf.
-Samuel Packwood qualified as Justice of the Peace
COURT, Samuel Clark, Edward Tatum, Joshua Rentfro, Samuel Packwood.. absent: A. Hughes, Francis Turner, Charles Thomas.
-Lawson vs Garrett
-McAlexander vs Mayberry
-Donaldson vs Smith exors.
-Ogle vs Boyd
-Bryant vs Hall
-Bridgeman vs Collings
-Burnett vs Henry - dismd
-Sutherland vs Tuggle
-Koger vs Posey, jury sworn: Joseph Willis, Jesse Tatum, Henry Smith, George Rogers, James Lyon, David Rogers, John Hughes, George Corn, John Tuggle, David Morgan, Samuel Dalton, Gabriel Penn..verdict returned for Defendant.
-David Rogers 2 days witness Stephen Lyon vs William Gilliam
-Jesse Tatum 2 days for same
-Abraham Frazor 2 days for same
-Hall vs Lawson - dismd
-Lawson vs Hall - dismd
-Harris vs Turner - dismd

PAGE 136

-Dean vs Smith, to be redocketed
-Jesse Tatum allowed $70.00 for services as Commissioner for the year 1796.
-James Baker 1 day and 25 miles coming and returning as witness Henry Koger vs Humphrey Posey
-Henry Sumpter 1 day 25 miles for same
-John Dillard 1 day for same
-Coss Abraham vs Vest..referred to Joseph Jessop and Jesse Corn.
-Joseph Miller 1 day and 27 miles Henry Koger vs Humphrey Posey
-Daniel Brileman(Prillaman) 1 day 25 miles for same
-Hugh Martin 1 day and 35 miles for same
-Samuel Packwood 1 day for same

COURT Saturday 30 July 1796 present: Brett Stovall, Samuel Packwood, Gabriel Penn, Abraham Penn, Joshua Rentfro, John Breden Jr.

-Breden vs Maberry Jr, jury sworn: Edward Lewis, William Lindsay, Gabriel Penn, Thomas Cooper, John Dalton, John Ferrell, Robert Scott, Robert Rowan, William Keaton, Joseph Keaton, Zackeriah Keaton, William Fitzgerald..verdict for Defendant.
-Lewis vs Going, referred to Brett Stovall and Joshua Rentfro
-Breden vs Morgan, Pltf to take deposition of the Auditor of Publick Accounts.
-Brown vs Brooks, jury sworn: Thomas Cooper, Gabriel Penn, Andrew Breden, John Ferrell, Zachariah Keaton, William Keaton, Joseph Keaton, William Lindsay, Joseph Rea Johnson, James Taylor, John Collings, John Dalton..verdict for the Pltf.
-Helton vs Tuggle, jury sworn: Thomas Cooper, Gabriel Penn, Andrew Breden, John Ferrell, Zachariah Keaton, William Keaton, Joseph Keaton, William Lindsay, Joseph R. Johnson, James Taylor, John Collings, John Dalton..verdict returned for Pltf.

PAGE 137

-Smith vs Shelton, jury sworn: Thomas Cooper, John Fletcher, James Taylor, John Dalton, Isaac Dodson, Andrew Breden, Joseph Keaton, William Keaton, John Collings, William Fitzgerald, Edward Lewis, Joseph Going..a juror withdrew and continued.
-William Adams 1 day witness Hall vs Lawson
-John Koger, William Sharp and David Morgan are appointed Commissioners to value property.
-Burnett Sr vs Mayberry and others..the Defendant James Lackey came into Court and confessed Judgement according to specialty and costs, a stay until Christmas next.
-Morgan vs Breden
-John Fletcher 3 days witness Levey Smith vs Eliphaz Shelton
-James Lyon 1 day for same
-A view of a road from Taylorsville to James Lyons returned.
-Lyon vs Smith - redocket

County of Patrick for year 1796

Clerks annual salary	25.
Sheriffs annual salary	25.
Deputy States Attorney annual salary	25.

-A negro slave named Peter, property of Samuel Clark, is exempt from the payment of levies for the future
-Eliphaz Shelton 1 day witness Coss Abram vs Vest
-Gabriel Penn 1 day for same
-Gabriel Penn 2 days witness Levy Smith vs Eliphaz Shelton
-Adams vs Keaton

PAGE 138

COURT Thursday 25 August 1796 present: Charles Thomas, Joshua Rentfro, Francis Turner, John Breden.

-Deed- Zaphaniah Tenison to Isham Cradock
-Deed- Samuel Waggoner to Charles Perkins
-Elisabeth Wells relinquishes her right of dower to a deed conveyed by her husband to Richard Thomas
-Deed of Trust Daniel Frans Jr to William Banks
-Hairston vs Abbington
-Hughes vs McCain
-Moore vs West, Samuel Staples security for costs
-Saunders vs Henry
-Sutherland vs Tuggle
-Amos Coombs 1 day 25 miles witness John Tuggle vs Alexander Sutherland
-Heath vs Sharp
-Sutton vs Tatum
-Heath vs Chitwood
-Heath vs Hollandsworth
-Heath vs Godard
-Morgan vs Walter
-Ordered that the Sheriff be enjoined from collecting a claim of Richard Adkinson of 22/10 from Roda Moore, which was allowed him for his attendance at a Court after Judgement was obtained vs Griffin.
-Deed- Abraham Edes to Mathew Moore
-Deed- Eliphaz Shelton to Robert Rowan and Robert Scott, Ann Shelton wife of Eliphaz Shelton relinquishes her right of dower
-William James Mayo, Valentine Mayo, Samuel Layne, James Morrison or any 3 to view a way for a road from Major Hancocks old cabin into the road leading from Francis Turners to the Patrick Courthouse and report.
-William J. Mayo, John Turner, Beveridge Hughes and William Burnett or any three view a way for a road from John Turners to the top of the Bull Mountain and report.

PAGE 139

-John Tatum presented a list of insolvents to the Court for the year 1794 and was allowed 228 for the same.
-John Ellison appeared in Court and refused to act as Justice of the Peace for the County.
COURT Thursday 29 September 1796 present: James Lyon, William Banks, Hamon Critz, Joshua Rentfro
-Last Will and Testament of Thomas Harbour was exhibited and ordered recorded.
-Gabriel Penn son of Philip Penn is recommended as a fit person to serve as Lt. of Militia in place of Charles Crutcher.
-William Witt as Ensign in place of Gabriel Penn
-William Pilson appointed surveyor of the road from Francis Turners to the foot of the Mountain in room of William Burnett.
-Overseers of the Poor to bind out George Daniel, Joyce Daniel, Fanny Daniel, Stephen Daniel, James Commings, Moses Commings and Joseph Commings according to Law.
-Deed- Pleasant Sowell to George Hairston
-Gabriel Penn, jailor of this County, produced his accounts for guarding and dieting Martin Dunkin, allowed 16½ for same.
-Deed- Thomas Man ?? to Michael McDearman
-George Carter, Eliphaz Shelton, Harvey Fitzgerald, Robert Sharp or any three to view a way for a road from Patrick Courthouse to Joshua Adams and from said Adams to the Montgomery line near Pattersons Quarter and report.

PAGE 140

The County Levey for 1796, brt fwd	75.0.0
To William Green, 3 young wolf heads	6.24
To John Christian for same	6.24
To Rowan & Scott for B. Belcher, 1 old wolf head	4.16
To Jesse Corn 1 old wolf head	4.16
To Samuel Corn same	4.16
To Charles Foster same	4.16
To Alexander Lackey 12 hrs patroll	.75
To Andrew Breden same	.75
To Richard Pilson same	.75
To Gabriel Penn as Goalor	5.0
To William Willis, jury on body of S. Rickman	1.5
To Alexander Lackey, 16 hours patroll	1.0
To Andrew Breden same	1.0
To Richard Pilson, 9 hours patroll	.55
To William Carter, processioning land 9 days	4.50
To B. M. Price for 30 days same	15.0
To John Tatum, 9 days for same	4.50
To Charles Thomas, 20 days for same	10.
To Augustine Thomas, 6 days for same	3.
To George Penn	11.
To Rodah Moore	6.50
To William Fuson	2.0
To David Harbour	9.0
To Samuel Staples, assignee of W. J. Mayo	26.50
To William Green	7.0
To Jacob Critz	4.50
To James Taylor	11.50
To James Turner	4.50
To James Lyon Jr	7.0
To William Willis	14.0
To Samuel Clark Jr	9.0
To Thomas Whitlock	8.50
To Nathaniel Smith	12.50
To Eliphaz Shelton for iron furnished for Jail	2.50
To Samuel Staples, Clerk	40.0
To Joseph R. Johnson, 12 days processioning	6.0
	333.97

PAGE 141

COURT September 1796

-On the motion of William P. Branham by his attorney to stay the proceedings and judgement of Elisabeth Laurence, his security is William Branham Sr.
-Joseph Comming sworn as Constable
-Gilliam vs Newman, Nathaniel Smith his security
-Ross vs Walters, dismd
-Sutton vs Tatum, dismd
-Heath vs Hollandsworth, dismd
-Heath vs Godard, N.P.
-Going vs Penn dismd
-Jesse Tatum appointed Commissioner for this County
-List of insolvent land returned by David Hanby for 1795
-Another list amounting to 68 tithes
-Also 3 other lists of same kind by A. Hughes
-A view of a way for a road from Major Hancocks old cabin to a road leading from Francis Turners to Patrick Courthouse returned and ordered that David Harbour and his gang do clear same.
-Also a view of a road from Francis Turners to the top of Bull Mtn was returned.. ordered William James Mayo and William Pilsons hands clear the same.

PAGE 142

COURT Thursday 27 October 1796 present: Charles Foster, Francis Turner, Gabriel Penn, Charles Thomas.

-Deed- John Douglas to Peter Bellow, Martha Douglas, wife of John, relinquishes her right of dower
-Deed- Henry France to Augustine Thomas
-Deed- Abraham Eads to William Carter
-Cradock vs Tenison, Edward Lewis Spl Bl
-Deed- Joel Appling to Rodah Moore, Mary Appling wife of Joel Appling relinquishes her right of dower
-John Tatum foreman, William Sharp, Nathaniel N. Helton, William McAlexander, James Bartlett, James Pigg, George Dodson Sr, Samuel Kennon, Thomas Dillard, Jesse Tatum, Jr, Edmund Chitwood, Joseph Johnson, Joshua Haynes, Nehemiah Daniel, Humphrey Smith, Nathaniel Ross were sworn as Grand Jury.
-Rowark vs William Henslee - dismd
-Thomas Roe Hall qualified as Ensign of the Militia
-Deed- Pleasant Sowell to George Hairston
-Tatum assignee vs Adams, jury sworn: John Douglas, Moses Reynolds, George Fulcher, William Fuson, James Turner, William Moore, John Fletcher, Beveridge Hughes, Henry Thompson, Andrew Breden, Joseph Reynolds and David Taylor..verdict for Defendant..new tryall granted Pltf on payment of costs.
-Deed- Anthony Tittle to George Hairston..Nancy Tittle, wife of Anthony Tittle, relinquishes her right of dower
-Humphrey Smith appeared in Court-----the Peace against Marvel Bolling, whereupon Marvel Bolling with Micajah Burnett, Richard Bolling and George Lackey his security...said Marvel Bolling to be of good behavior 12 months 1 day towards Humphrey Smith.
-Adkinson vs Ross
-Adams vs Corn - dismd

PAGE 143

-Benjamin Cloud recommended as Lt. in place of Martin Dickerson who hath resigned. Joseph R. Johnson as Ensign in place of Benjamin Cloud.
-The Order of the last Court relative to the recommending of Gabriel Penn and William Witt is rescinded.. William Witt as Ensign in place of G. Penn who refused to Act.
-Lewis vs Eckolds
-Adam Tittle is allowed 2 days witness Jacob Adams Sr vs John Tatum.

Page 143 contd

COURT Friday 28 October 1796 present: James Lyon, Francis Turner, Charles Foster, Brett Stovall

-McAlexander vs Mabury Jr..judgement granted for Pltf.
-Donaldson vs Smith executor of Deweese
-Ogle vs Boyd
-Bryant vs Hall
-Garrett vs Lawson and wife
-Bridgman vs Colling
-Dean vs Smith
-Breden vs Morgan
-Philpott vs Koger: deposition of Samuel Hunter to be taken.
-Lyon vs Smith: deposition of R. N. Venable and Thomas Mitchell to be taken.

PAGE 144

-Smith vs Shelton: jury sworn: Barnard M. Price, Richard Tucker Mayner, Humphrey Smith, Humphrey Posey, Stanwix Hord, John Medley Sr, William Callem, Greensville Penn, James Turner, James Randals, Philip Penn, James Baker..verdict returned for Pltf, the negro man Charles alias Jack in the declaration mentioned, if to be had, if not Ł150. the value of him and one cent damages.
-Bryant vs Hall, deposition of Augustine Brown to be taken
-David Tittle, 1 day witness Hall vs Bryant
-Augustine Brown 1 day for same
-Stanwix Hord 1 day and 25 miles witness Samuel Philpott vs Henry Koger.
-James Baker same
-Samuel Hunter same
-Humphrey Posey 1 day for same
-Nathan Harris 1 day for same
-William Consolvent 1 day for same
-Jeremiah Stone 1 day and 26 miles for same
-David Rogers 1 day witness Gilliam vs Newman
-Boles vs Smallman
-Humphrey Posey 1 day witness Bryant vs Hall
-Gilliam vs Newman
-Adams vs Keaton

PAGE 145

COURT Thursday 24 November 1796 present: James Lyon, Samuel Clark, Charles Foster, Joshua Rentfro

-Deed- Francis Graham to George Hairston
-On a motion of James Turner by his attorney for a Judgement against Daniel Carlin, late Sheriff, for a balance of deposit in his hands for the years 1794 and 1795. Judgement granted for $15.50.
-Deed of Trust- Joseph Newman to Gabriel Penn
-Saunders vs Nowlin(Nolen)
-Deed- Robert Hall to John Sharp Sr
-Hairston vs Abington
-Hughes vs McCain
-Moore vs West
-Heath vs Godard
-Boles vs Smallman
-Sutton vs Tatum
-Hall vs Vest
-Tatum vs Going
-Hairston vs Devenshire
-Breden vs Lackey
-Lindsay vs Clark
-Smith vs Bolling
-Deed- William Hanner to Samuel Clark
-Koger vs Philpott, depo of Nancy Slater and Daniel Slater and Mrs. Slater to be taken.

Page 145 contd

-Smith vs Bolling, deposition of Richard Burnett to be taken.

PAGE 146

COURT Thursday 29 December 1796 present: James Lyon, John Breden, Edward Tatum, George Penn

-Deed- George Garrett to William Garrett
-Saunders vs Jeremiah Burnett Jr, dismd
-Deed- Henry Smith and wife to William Smith Jr
-Deed of Trust - Joseph Newman to Gabriel Penn
-Going vs Medley, dismd
-Robert Sharp appointed surveyor of the road from the forks of the road below Tatums to the forks below David Hanby and opposite Robert Hall in place of G. Davidson.
-Adams vs Keaton, referred to William Banks and Joshua Rentfro
-Deed- James Lyon to Benjamin Philpott
-Reynolds vs Keaton
-Hairston vs Abington
-Moore vs West
-Hughes vs McCain, abates by the death of Pltf.
-Boles vs Smallman
-Sutton vs Tatum
-Saunders vs Lewis N.P.
-Saunders vs Nowlin
-Hall vs Vest
-Hairston vs Devenshire
-Breden vs Lackey
-Foley vs Smith
-Lindsay vs Clark
-Tatum vs Going
-Jesse Corn allowed 1 day witness Andrew Breden vs J. Lackey

PAGE 147

COURT Thursday 26 January 1797 present: Samuel Clark, William Banks, Thomas Whitlock and Joshua Rentfro.

County Levey for 1796 brt fwd	333.97
to Samuel Staples for service	20.
Depositium for use of County	50.
Sheriff collect $403.97 by 888 tythables	
@ 48 cents per poll	428.20

-Deed- Daniel France to William Banks
-Saunders vs Joseph Adams
-Charles Foster, Charles Thomas and Samuel Packwood to settle the accounts current of the estate of John Lackey, dec'd.
-Burgess Brammer appointed surveyor of the road in place of John Hall.
-Francis Turner, Thomas Morrow, Beveridge Hughes and Moses Hurt to view a way to turn the road leading through the lands of Jeremiah Burnett Sr and William Burnett.
-James Lyon Jr appointed surveyor of the road in place of John Fletcher.
-Hall vs Vess
-Saunders vs James Nowlin
-An instrument of writing between William Hamblett and William Barton was recorded.
-Smith vs Bolling
-John Lemmings ?? exempt from the payment of County and Parish levies for the future.
-Power of attorney of James Fulkerson to John Hanby
-Administration of the estate of Archelaus Hughes dec'd, is granted Mary Hughes the widow and relict, and John Hughes with securities: Jonathan Hanby, William Carter, Thomas Mitchell, William Lindsay, Gabriel Penn and Peter Scales.
-Joshua Rentfro, Joseph Stovall, Richard Mills to appriase estate.

PAGE 148

-Edward Lewis an invalid pensioner, his pension to continue at 15 pounds.
-Branham vs Laurence
-Power of attorney of Francis Turner to William McPeak
-Hairston vs Abington
-Boles vs Smallman N.P.

COURT Thursday 23 February 1797 present: James Lyon, Francis Turner, Edward Tatum and Charles Thomas.

-Deed- William Nowlin to John Medley Jr
-Bill of Sale, John Sharp Sr to Thomas Mitchell
-Bill of Sale, William Lindsay to George Carter
-James Taylor foreman, William McAlexander, Isham Cradock, Humphrey Smith, William Frazior, John Chitwood, James Ferrell, John F. Camron, James Turner, John Tatum, George Rogers, Jesse Lewis, John Hall are sworn as Grand Jury.
-John Wilson sworn as Constable
-Samuel Hanby qualified as Deputy Sheriff
-Elijah Dehart with his security Richard Burnett a Bond..for 4 years @ 8 pounds per annum to keep the Overseers of the Poor from all costs that might arise in consequence of his having two bastard children begotten on the body of Sarah Vest.

PAGE 149

-Deed- William Adams to William Lindsay
-Lewis vs Peregoy
-Administration of the estate of Samuel King is granted Isham Cradock.
-John Koger, Zaphaniah Tenison, Barnard M. Price, Jacob Adams are to appraise said estate of Samuel King.
-Jonathan Hanby with securities William Carter, Samuel Staples, Thomas Mitchell, Robert Scott and Edward Tatum to collect the tax for the year 1796.
-Newman vs Lyon, William Adams Spl Bl
-Saunders vs Lewis, Isham Cradock, Spl Bl
-Burnett Jr vs Maberry & Turner, dismd
-Hanby vs Green
-Hall vs Vest

PAGE 150

COURT Friday 24 February 1797 present: Francis Turner, Charles Thomas, Charles Foster, Gabriel Penn, John Breden Jr

-Cradock vs Tenison, referred to Samuel Hairston and Edward Tatum.
-On a motion of Elijah Dehart to set aside the recognizance entered into yesterday for his indemnifing the Overseers of the Poor from the charge of two bastard children begotten on the body of Sarah Vest, on hearing the arguments on both sides, the Court were of the opinion that the proceedings were illegal, therefore recognizance dismissed.
-Smith vs Bolling
-Deed- Stanwix Hord to Abel Perigoy
-Jesse Corn 2 days witness Marvel Bolling vs Humphrey Smith
-William Frazior 2 days for same
-Adkinson vs Ross
-Donaldson vs Smith, executor of Deweese
-Turman vs Kimzey referred to Charles Foster, Henry Harris, Bird Smith and Guy Smith.
-Ogle vs Boyd, jury sworn: William Frazior, John Sharp Jr, Edward Lewis, Joseph Going, Richard T. Maynor, Andrew Breden, William Fuson, Thomas R. Hall, John Medley Jr, David Harbour, Humphrey Smith,... verdict for Pltf.
-Saunders vs Stow, William Witt Spl Bl

Page 150 contd

-Bridgman vs Collings, jury sworn: John Dalton, Samuel Clark Jr, Peter Saunders, John Hughes, William Willis, Thomas Hudson, David Morgan, Moses Harbour, George Penn, Thomas Mitchell, Robert Sharp, John Hall. ..verdict for Pltf in amount of 5 cents.
-Deed- Luke Foley to William James Mayo
-Lyon vs Smith, jury sworn: Samuel Clark, Peter Saunders, William Willis, Robert Sharp, Thomas Hudson, David Morgan, Moses Harbour, George Penn, John Sharp, James Taylor, John Benion, John Medley Sr. Verdict for Pltf, fifty pounds damages.
-George Crawford 2 days witness H. Smith vs M. Bolling
-Nehemiah Bloomer 2 days and 30 miles witness for John Ogle vs James Boyd.

PAGE 151

-Bryant vs Hall
-Booker vs Maynor - dismd
-Gilliam vs Newman
-Going vs Keaton
-Rentfro assignee vs Tuggle, jury sworn: William Witt, David Harbour, John Hornsby, David Roberson, Daivd Ross, William Fuson, Edward Lewis, Daniel Adams, Joshua Adams, John Adams, William McPeak, Joseph Going. Verdict for Pltf in amount of 15 pounds.
-McPeak vs Hall, jury sworn: Edward Lewis, Joshua Adams, Daniel Adams, John Medley, Nathaniel Ross, David Ross, John Adams, Joseph Going, David Roberson, William Witt, David Harbour, John Hanby..a juror withdrew..W.E. set aside, not guilty and issue and continued.
-same vs McBride
-David Roberson 2 days witness Hall vs McPeak
-Francis Turner 2 days for same
-James Morrison 1 day for same
-William Fuson 1 day for same
-Bartlett Reynolds 2 days witness Samuel Philpott vs Henry Koger
-Edward Tatum 2 days witness James Lyon vs Nathaniel Smith
-Thomas Mitchell 1 day for same
-William McPeak 2 days witness William Turman vs Benjamin Kimzey

PAGE 152

COURT Saturday 25 February 1797 present: Edward Tatum, Abram Penn, Gabriel Penn, Samuel Packwood, Charles Foster, Charles Thomas.

-Deed- James McCain to John Chandler
-Lyon vs Smith, on an agreement -------Executors, same was overruled, and the verdict and Judgement be valid and good.
-Breden vs Morgan, jury sworn:Isaac Dodson, Edward Lewis, James Lackey, John Medley Jr, John Medley Sr, Daniel Adams, Samuel Clark, David Taylor, Samuel Philpott, Humphrey Smith, William James Mayo, Henry Koger..verdict for Pltf for 25 pounds, new tryal granted Defendant.
-Deed- Richard Adkinson to Laurence Lee, 2 deeds
-Deed- William Sowell to George Hairston
-Hill vs Penn, W.E. set aside, James Taylor Spl Bl
-Bristoe vs Morgan - dismd
-Breden vs Morgan
-Morgan vs Yeates - dismd
-McKinery or McKimzey vs Hairston
-Adams vs Foster
-Lewis vs Going
-Philpott vs Koger, jury sworn: Peter Saunders, William Willis, Jacob Michaux, John Mankin, Henry Smith, John Sharp, Isaac Dodson, James Taylor, Nathaniel Ross, David Ross, Andrew Breden, Thomas Mitchell. ..verdict for defendant
-James Baker 2 days and 20 miles Henry Koger vs Samuel Philpott
-Jeremiah Stone 2 days and 22 miles for same
-Stanwix Hord 2 days 21 miles for same
-Bartlett Reynolds 1 day for same
-Malacai Cummings 2 days for same

PAGE 153

-Nathan Harris 2 days witness Philpott vs Koger
-Polly Dority 3 days for same
-Nancy Sleator 3 days for same
-Peter Vess 2 days for same
-William T. Vaughan 2 days for same
-Jacob Adams Sr 3 days for same
-Stephen Consolvent 3 days for same
-William Willis 2 days for same
-Humphrey Posey 3 days for same
-A. Hughes 2 days for same
-John Tatum presented a list of insolvents for the year 1794 under Daniel Carlin, sheriff.
-Newman vs Lyon; A. Hughes and William Lindsay Spl Bl
-Tenison vs William Adams and Joshua Adams..on a motion of Complaintant by his attorney, the Defendant having failed to enter his appearing according to the Act of Assemby and ride.... of and it appearing to the Court that the said William Adams is not an inhabitant of this State. Ordered that the Defendant appear here at the next Quarterly Court to answer Complaint Bill and that a copy of this order be forthwith inscribed in the Virginia Gazette for 8 weeks and set up at the door of said Courthouse in the County of Patrick.
-Smith vs Corn and others in Chancery..the Defendant John Poteet and James Poteet not having entered their appearance and given security agreeable to the Act of Assembly and the rules of this Court. It is ordered that they appear at the next quarterly session.
-Sheriff to pay John Tatum 4 pounds 3 shillings 7 pence out of his account for the year 1795 and 1796.

PAGE 154

-Smith vs Taylor - dismd
-Rowan & Scott vs Samuel Philpott
-Tatum assignee vs Adams, jury sworn: Christopher Long, Robert Sharp, Peter Saunders, Thomas Mitchell, John Hanby, Arch. Shelton, Stephen Smith, Isaac Dodson, John Bennett, John Sharp, Humphrey Smith, Nathaniel Ross..verdict for Pltf.
-Peter Saunders 3 days and 27 miles witness John Tatum vs Jacob Adams
-Peter Saunders 3 days witness Peter Saunders Jr vs James Lackey

COURT Thursday 30 March 1797 present: Samuel Clark, Joshua Rentfro, Edward Tatum, Francis Turner, James Lyon.

-Charles Crutcher qualified as Lt. of Militia
-James Lyon and Daniel Carlin, late Sheriff, to Joshua Rentfro
-Deed- Peter Edwards attorney for John Hobson to William Gray
-Deed- Jesse Corn to William Gardner
-On a motion of Gabriel Penn, leave is granted him to keep an Ordinary at his home in the Town of Taylorsville, Joshua Rentfro his security.
-Deed- Charles Foster to Benjamin Hancock
-Deed- William Adams to William Lindsay
-Deed- John W. Watson to Samuel C. Morrison
-Blankenship vs Chitwood..Isham Blankenship security for costs
-Power of attorney of George Maberry Jr to James Lackey

PAGE 155

-Adams vs Tatum, dismd
-Tatum vs Going, dismd
-Sackville Brewer appointed surveyor of the road from Critz new buildings to Henry Lynes in place of Joseph Taylor.
-William Keaton appointed surveyor of the road from the ford of Spoon Creek above Hamon Critz to the line past above Shadrick Barretts old place.
-George Fulcher appointed surveyor of the road from Patrick Courthouse to Joseph Goings.

Page 155 contd

-Ordered that Mrs. Critz hands and John Millers be added to Jacob Critz list of hands.
-On a motion of William Gardner, ordered that a Writ -----issue to -------and a Jury to view a mill seat on his land and report.
-Samuel Staples the same
-A report of a view of a road thru the lands of Jeremiah Burnett was returned.
-Also a report of a view from Patrick Courthouse to Pattersons Quarter.
-William Willis appointed surveyor of the road from Obediah Hudsons to the Grayson line in place of Benjamin Garrett.

The Court doth set and rate the following:

Breakfast	0.1.3
Dinner	0.1.6
Supper	0.1.3
Lodgings	0.0.4
Corn and Oats per gallon	0.0.6
Sheave oats per bdl	0.0.2
Fodder	0.0.1
Rum, if Continental per gal.	1.16.0
West Indian or Antigo	0.04.
Brandy	0.12.
Whiskey	0.10.

-Joshua Adams is appointed to call on George Fulcher and his gang, Eliphaz Shelton and his, William Pilson and his and they are to clear and open a road from Patrick Courthouse to the Montgomery line near Pattersons Quarter.

PAGE 156

-Lackey vs Mayo, referred to John Tuggle and Henry Tuggle, Thomas Morgan, John Conner or any three of them.
-William Carter, William Banks, Charles Foster and George Penn or any three appointed to settle with the different Sheriffs since the commencement of this County and report.
-William Banks, Joshua Rentfro and Edward Tatum are appointed to examine the Clerks and Surveyors office and report to June Court.
-Administration of the estate of John Smallman dec'd is granted to Mary Smallman widow and relict with Moses Godward her security.
-Samuel Packwood, George Reaves, Richard T. Maynor and James Commings to appraise said estate.
-Moore vs West, Judgement for Def.
-Boles vs Smallman, non-suit
-William James Mayo qualified as Deputy Clerk
-Sutton vs Tatum
-Tatum v Going, dismd
-Lyon vs Philpott, Judgement
-Foley vs Smith, Judgement
-Lewis vs Lackey, same
-Breden vs Lackey same
-Hairston vs Devonshire, contd
-Staples vs Keaton, Judgement for the Defendant
-John Gates 1 day witness Joseph Keaton vs Samuel Staples
-Benjamin Hale 1 day for same

PAGE 157

COURT Thursday 27 April 1797 present: Samuel Clark, Edward Tatum, Francis Turner, Charles Thomas.

-Deed- John Brammer to Thomas Plaster
-Deed- Peter Edwards attorney for John Hobson to William Gray
-Deed- Edmund Brammer to Aron Williams
-Deed- Anthony Tittle to Thomas W. Ruble
-Deed- Abraham Mayse to James Hollandsworth

Page 157 contd

-Deed- Isaac Hollandsworth to Abraham Mayse and James Hollandsworth
-Deed- William B. Parmer to Elisabeth Laurence
-Deed- James Sleator to Daniel Sleator
-Deed- Edward Daniel to Robert Stockton
-Deed- James Harris and others to Samuel Harris
-Deed- John Daniel to Richard Massey
-Deed- Humphrey Posey to William King
-Deed- John Jones and wife to Hieron Wills
-Deed- William Allen to Peter Stolts
-Deed- Palmer Scritchfield to Spencer Talley
-Deed- Andrew Polson to Peter Hale
-Humphrey Smith foreman, John Turner, Simon Dodson,David Morgan, Richard Thomas, Thomas Dillard, Samuel Clark Jr, Richard Massey, Richard T. Maynor, Isham Cradock, John Creed, Robert Hudspeth, Nathaniel N.Helton, John Lee, Jeremiah Jadwin and Job Ross to serve as Grand Jury.
-Deed of Trust- John Chandler to Samuel Staples
-Deed- Abraham Penn and John Medley Sr to John Medley Jr
-Deed- John W. Watson to Samuel C. Morris

PAGE 158

-Deed- Ignatious Redman and wife to George Hairston
-Hughes Admn. vs Frans

COURT Friday 28 April 1797 present: William Carter, Joshua Rentfro, William Banks, Charles Foster, Francis Turner, Charles Thomas.

-Deed- Sarah Harris, James Harris andother to Samuel Harris
-Saunders vs Lackey, David Morgan Spl Bl also Alexander Lackey Spl Bl
-Sams vs Lee, Charles Foster Spl Bl, William Fuson further Spl Bl
-Power of attorney of Humphrey Smith executor of Cornelius Deweese dec'd to David Morgan
-Deed of Trust- Benjamin Philpott to Samuel Staples
-Adkinson vs Ross, jury sworn: John Lee, John Hall, John Turman, Zaphaniah Tenison, William McAlexander, Samuel Harris, David Keaton, David Morgan, Nathan Hall, Moses Reynolds, Samuel Clark Jr, H. Smith. A juror withdrew and continued.
-Coss Abraham a free negro vs Vest, referred to Jesse Corn and William Banks.
-Donaldson vs Smith executor of Deweese, contd
-Bryant vs Hall, dismd
-Gilliam vs Newman
-Going vs Keaton, dismd

PAGE 159

-McPeak vs Hall, dismd
-McPeak vs McBride and wife, dismd
-Blankenship vs Chitwood, Joshua Rentfro Spl Bl
-David Roberson 1 day witness Hall vs McPeak
-James Morrison 1 day for same
-Coss Abraham a free negro vs Vest, verdict for Pltf sum of $25.00
-Breden vs Morgan, contd
-Morgan vs Breden, contd
-McKinnery vs Hairston, dismd
-Adams vs Foster, contd
-John Henry 1 day and 38 miles as witness David Morgan vs Andrew Breden
-Hayse vs Maynor
-Morgan vs Breden
-Blankenship vs Chitwood
-Philpott vs Lyon, jury sworn: Alexander Lackey, William McAlexander, William Sloane, Moses Reynolds, Samuel Harris, Joseph Going, David Morgan, Humphrey Smith, James Taylor, Stephen Adkinson, John Lee, Joshua Adams...verdict for Defendant
-Hill vs Penn
-McPeak vs Hall, jury sworn: Alexander Lackey, William McAlexander,

Page 159 contd

William Sloan, Moses Reynolds, Elijah Banks, Joseph Going, Daniel Adams, James Taylor, William Adams, John Lee, Joshua Adams..verdict for Defendant.
-James Lackey 1 day witness John Hall vs McPeak
-William Fuson 1 day for same

PAGE 160

-Blankenship vs Chitwood, take deposition of Christopher Clark.
-George Fulcher 1 day witness Philpott vs Lyon
-Elisha Blankenship 1 day 50 miles witness Blankenship vs Chitwood
-Francis Turner 1 day witness Hall vs McPeak
-Philpott vs Penn, jury sworn: James Taylor, William Sloan, Alexander Lackey, Jacob Saunders, William Adams, William McAlexander, James Lackey, Joshua Adams, David Morgan, Moses Reynolds, John Henry, Joseph Going...verdict for Defendant, new tryal granted Plaintiff.
-McGowan vs Boyd
-Newman vs Lyon, jury sworn: James Taylor, William Sloan, Alexander Lackey, Jacob Saunders, William McAlexander, John Henry, David Morgan, William Adams, Moses Reynolds, Joseph Going, Joshua Adams, Joel Chitwood..verdict returned for Pltf.
-Rowan & Scott vs Philpott..same jury as above..verdict returned for the Pltf.
-Smith vs Vest
-Walter vs Ogle

PAGE 161

COURT Thursday 25 May 1797 present: William Carter, Edward Tatum, John Breden, Samuel Clark, James Lyon, Joshua Rentfro.

-Deed- Robert Pennington to Elijah Dehart
-Deed- Isaac Hollandsworth to Zachariah King
-On a motion of Rowan & Scott leave is granted them to keep an Ordinary at their house in Taylorsville.
-Deed- Susannah Marr to Joseph Pennington
-Deed- Susannah Clark to Bartus Reynolds
-Samuel Philpott is appointed surveyor of the road from the top of Bull Mtn to Tanseys Path where it crosses the Bull Mtn Rd in place of Moses Godward.
-Ordered that William Pilson be discontinued from opening and closing the road from the Patrick Courthouse to Pattersons Quarter.
-Brett Stovall is admitted as one of the Administrators of the estate of Archelaus Hughes dec'd in addition to the others.
-Commonwealth vs Surveyors of the Road from the cross road below the Patrick Courthouse to James Taylors...dismd.
-Deed- William Hudspeth to John Creed
-Sutton vs Tatum, Judgement
-Dehart assignee vs Henry
-Hall vs Henry, Judgement
-Keaton vs Going
-Edmund Winston vs Newman
-Hall vs Moner ??
-Jones assignee vs Lewis
-Boles vs Smallman Administrators
-William Adams 1 day witness Joseph Keaton vs Joseph Going
-Callaway vs Mankins

PAGE 162

-John Hunter 1 day witness James Bowls vs Nancy Smallman
-Simon Dodson 1 day for same
-Joseph Commings 1 day for same
-Hairston vs Devonshire - contd
-Lackey vs McBride
-Daberey vs Hall

Page 162 contd

-Stewart vs Hall
-Chitwood vs Rickman, Court of the opinion that the property attached belongs to Peter Rickman and to be released.
-On the motion of Laughlin Fagin, leave is granted him to keep an Ordinary at his house in the County with John Tatum his security.
-Creed vs Johnson, Judgement in the sum of $12.00
-Cummings vs Going, referred to John Fletcher and Moses Reynolds
-Chitwood vs Rickman, dismd

COURT Thursday June 1797 present: Joseph Stovall, Samuel Clark, Charles Thomas, Joshua Rentfro, James Lyon

-James Patterson, Gentleman, produced in Court a license admitting him to practice Law in this and other Courts.
-A release or quit claim to a certain piece of land from Charles Crutcher to his mother Elisabeth Crutcher recorded.
-Deed- William B. Parmer to Elisabeth Laurence, further proved
-Keaton vs Going, referred to William Banks and George Penn
-Dehart assignee vs Henry, dismd

PAGE 163

-Thomas B. Jones vs Lewis, Judgement
-Boles vs Smallman Administrators, dismd
-Deed- Thomas Ward toJohn Lee, 2 deeds
-Simon Dodson 1 day witness Boles vs Smallman
-Joseph Cummings 1 day for same
-James Baker 1 day and 20 miles for same
-Dabney vs Hall, Judgement
-Adams vs Going, dismd
-Deed- John Adams to Elias Bryant
-Stewart vs Hall, Judgement
-Hairston vs Devonshire, contd
-Penn vs Tuggle, Judgement
-Penn vs Going
-Hall vs Maberry Jr, Judgement, William Burnett a garnishee
-Huges Adms vs Going

PAGE 164

COURT Thursday 27 July 1797 present: Charles Thomas, Charles Foster, Francis Turner, Brett Stovall, George Penn.

-Deed- Thomas McDonald to William Sloan
-Deed- Samuel Henry to Isham Burnett
-Deed- Misheck Perdue to James Ferrell
-Turman vs Kimzey, redocket
-Cummings vs Going
-A negro man named George (slave) the property of Charles Foster is exempt from levies for the future.
-Deed- Thomas Ward to John Lee, 2 deeds, further proved
-James Turner, James Fulkerson, Christopher Long, Humphrey Smith, James Taylor foreman, Peter Frans, Samuel Clark Jr, Augustine Thomas, Moses Reynolds, John Hughes, Nathaniel N. Helton, Daniel Morgan, Richard Thomas, Jesse Corn, William Gardner and Samuel Lane are sworn as Grand Jury.
-Breden vs Morgan, referred to George Penn, Joseph Reynolds,Thomas Goodson, Andrew McEnry, Samuel Eason
-Morgan vs Breden, referred to same as above
-Adkinson vs Ross, jury sworn: Thomas Mitchell, David Harbour, Elijah Banks, James Bartlett, John Medley Sr, William Lindsay, Andrew Breden, Clement Rogers, Obadiah Fields, Larkin Price, Elijah Dehart, Joel Willis..verdict for Pltf in amount of one cent.
-Donaldson vs Smith executor - dismd

PAGE 165

COURT, present: James Lyon, Hamon Critz, Samuel Clark, Stephen Lyon, Edward Tatum, Joseph Stovall.

-Samuel Clark, William Carter and Stephen Lyon are recommended as proper persons to serve as Sheriff.
-Absent: James Lyon, Hamon Critz, Joseph Stovall, Brett Stovall, Joshua Rentfro.

-Ordered that the Clerk of the County certify to the Executive an accurate account of the Acting Magistrate of this County agreeable to the Order of Council.

-Hughes Admn. vs Gilbert,James Thompson Spl Bl
-same vs Ward, Judgement
-Thomas B. Jones vs Lewis, Judgement set aside
-Thomas B. Jones executors vs Thomas Jones
-Gilliam vs Newman, jury sworn: Edward Lewis, James Fulkerson, Jesse Corn, Andrew Breden, John Breden, John Benion, James Taylor, William Burnett, Obadiah Dodson, Augustine Thomas, John Greenwood, Clement Rogers. A juror withdrew and continued.
-Deed- George Hairston to Adrian Anglin, 2 deeds
-Saunders vs Lee, William Fuson Spl Bl
-Charles Thomas, William Fuson, Charles Foster are appointed to settle the accounts of Cornelius Deweese with H. Smith, the executor.
-John Henry 1 day 38 miles witness David Morgan vs Andrew Breden.

PAGE 166

COURT Friday 28 July 1797 present: Francis Turner, James Lyon, Joshua Rentfro, Abraham Penn, Charles Thomas.

-On a motion of Daniel Carlin, late Sheriff, an injunction to stay the proceedings by James Turner,...over ruled.
-Penn vs Going, dismd
-Adams vs Foster, jury sworn: James Finney, James Taylor, James Turner, Archelaus Hughes, James Fulkerson, Samuel Clark Jr, Jesse Tatum, James Frost, Thomas Mitchell, John Sharp, David Taylor, Larkin Price.. a juror withdrew and continued.
-Elisha Blankenship 2 days 50 miles as witness Chitwood vs Blankenship.
-Saunders vs Stoe, jury sworn: Gabriel Penn, William Keaton, William Branham, John Dalton, H. Smith, Greensivlle Penn, Joseph Going, Edward Lewis, John Smith, Moses Reynolds, Archibald Shelton, Beveridge Hughes..verdict for Pltf in amount of one penny.

-Same vs Lackey, contd
-McGowan vs Boyd, dismd
-Fletcher vs Dodson, John Tatum Spl Bl
-Smith vs Vest
-Smith vs Carlin
-A negro man slave named Watt, the property of Samuel Clark, is exempt from the payment of further county and parish levies.
-Harvey Fitzgerald 1 day witness Commings vs Going

PAGE 167

COURT Thursday 31 August 1797 present: George Penn, Abraham Penn, James Lyon, Francis Turner, Munford Smith.

-James Thomason, Augustine Thomas, John Fletcher and Arthur Parr are appointed to view a way for a road from the HollowRd below John Parr into the Courthouse Rd below Bartons Plantation.
-Deed- Martin Martin to David Crew
-Hairston vs Devonshire, contd
-Deed- Francis Turner to Thomas P. Jordon
-Harris vs Tuggle, Judgement
-Hughes Admn vs Corn, Judgement

Page 167 contd

-Inventory of the estate of John Smallman returned
-Laughlin Fagin is appointed surveyor of the road from the ford of the Little Dan to Peters Creek at the mouth of Hanbys Lane.
-Salsberry vs Breden, Judgement
-William Robertson 1 day witness Salsberry vs Breden
-Henry Thompson 1 day for same
-Stewart vs Lackey, Judgement
-Wade vs Banks, contd
-Hatcher vs Brewer, Judgement
-Nathan Shelton 1 day 16 miles witness Hatcher vs Brewer
-Deed- Munford Smith, Jonathan Hanby andWilliam Carter to Jonathan Hanby.
-Wade vs Banks, referred to John Dillard
-Boyd vs Yoes, contd

PAGE 168

-John Turner, David Robertson, Isham Burnett and Mathew Moore are appointed to view a way for a road from John Turners to the top of Bull Mtn Rd leading to Patrick Courthouse.

Present: James Lyon, Samuel Clark, William Banks, Francis Turner, Charles Foster, Edward Tatum, Munford Smith, Joshua Rentfro, George Penn, Abraham Penn and William Carter.

Ordered that the former Order of the Court for the recommendation of Charles Foster as Captain of the Militia be rescinded.
-Gabriel Penn and John Hughes are recommended as fit and proper persons to serve in the Commission of the Peace for this County.
-Benjamin Cloud is recommended as Lt. of Militia 2nd Btn in place of Martin Dickerson.
-Mitchell Thompson is recommended as Ensign of the Militia
-Lindsay assignee vs Keaton
-William Fitzgerald 1 day witness Going vs Keaton
-John Wilson is recommended as Ensign in place of Munford Smith in the 2nd Btn of Militia
-On a motion of John Hall by his attorney for a Judgement on a delivery bond vs Ezekiel Morris and John Turman. Court of the opinion that the Judgement be awarded vs Morris the Defendant with costs.
-On a motion of Andrew Breden, Judgement also granted him vs Ezekiah Morris and James Lackey.
-John Creed, Bartlett Smith, John Christian and John Nunn or any three to view a way for a road from Platts Cabin on Little Dan River to the top of the Mountain at the Grayson line.
-Moore vs Clark, referred to James Lyon, Joshua Rentfro and their opinion is that of the Court.
-David Hanby allowed 45 miles for riding for attending to compair the polles of the election; also 45 miles for Congress and 60 miles for the Senate; also for summoning a called Court on a Felony.

PAGE 169

COURT Thursday 28 September 1797 present: Francis Turner, Edward Tatum, Joseph Stovall, Samuel Clark, Charles Thomas.

-Ordered that the Overseers of the Poor bind out Margaret Burser.???. (could be Burress) an orphan girl to David Rogers.
-Deed- Daniel Sleator to George Hairston
-Deed- George Dodson to Robert Lockhart
-Deed- John Loyd to John Fields
-Deed- Thomas Bristoe to Featherston Walden
-Power of attorney of William Price and Mary Price to Barnard M.Price
-Nathan Morrison is appointed Constable
-Deed- William Carter to George Hairston
-William Ogle appeared in Court and conefssed that in a fight he bit off a part of the ear of John Johnson.

Page 169 contd

-Deed- Jonathan Hanby to John Hanby
-Deed- John Benion to Jesse Reynolds
-Hairston vs Devonshire
-Jesse Tatum presented a list of taxable property for the year 1797.
-Keaton vs Going, Award executed
-Stewart vs Lackey, Judgement
-Staples & Co vs Rickman, Judgement
-Staples & Co vs Shelton, dismd
-Byd (Bryd?) vs Yoes, contd

COURT, present: James Lyon, Charles Thomas, Joshua Rentfro, Samuel Packwood. Absent: Edward Tatum, Samuel Clark, Francis Turner.

-Edward Tatum is appointed Commissioner of this County.

PAGE 170

-Thomas Bolling allowed 1 day witness Shelton vs Staples & Company
-Henry Koger 1 day for same
-Jesse Tatum allowed $65.00 for his services rendered as Commissioner of this County.
-On a motion of Jonathan Hanby, Gentleman Sheriff, John Dalton is admitted as Deputy Sheriff.
-A list of land and property tax returned by Jonathan Hanby for 1796.

COURT Thursday 26 October 1797 present: James Lyon, Samuel Clark, William Banks, Joseph Stovall

-Hughes assignee vs Frans, Judgement
-Corn vs Oldham, Award for Defendant
-On a motion of Henry Koger leave is granted him to keep an Ordinary in the Town of Taylorsville with George Penn his security.
-Willis vs Fields, dismd
-Briscoe vs Mankin, Harvey Fitzgerald Spl Bl
-A report of a Writ of Adquadamnum between John Burnett and Micajah Burnett and Humphrey Smith was returned.
-James Taylor foreman, Jesse Corn, John Hall, Archelaus Hughes, Ezekiel Morris, William McAlexander, Humphrey Smith, Richard Thomas, Joshua Adams, Clement Rogers, Joel Willis, Moses Harbour, John Adams, John Ferrell, John Adams, John Breden Sr are to serve as Grand Jury.
-Davis vs Penington & Martindill, dismd
-Saunders vs Lackey
-Benjamin Haile allowed 2 days as witness for......

PAGE 171

-Commonwealth vs Hughes
-Commonwealth vs Adams
-Wade vs Banks
-Ross vs McNanney, Judgement
-Samuel Clark, Gentleman, produced a Commission appointing him Sheriff with securities: Samuel Staples, William Banks, Edward Tatum.
-Clark Jr vs Koger, dismd
-Adams vs Foster, Defendant confess Judgement for 75 pounds with interest from 18 Sept 1793 and cost of this suit. Also 43 pounds 10 shilling the cost of a suit in the District Court in the name of Secknight Lessee of Ward against Adams and the Plaintiff on his part agrees to relinquish all action or causes of actions or demands whatsoever against the said Defendant and his heirs and against Thomas Hoff and his heirs and the Plaintiff agrees to stay till 30 June next.
-Tenison vs Adams, dismd
-Nathan Hall is allowed 4 days witness Adams vs Foster
-Henry Peregoy 1 day for same
-Charles Thomas allowed 4 days for same
-Joseph Peregoy 1 day and 20 miles for same
-Acquilla Blackley 1 day and 50 miles for same

Page 171 contd

-Daniel Adams 4 days for same
-Robert Hall 1 day for same
-Bartlett Belcher 1 day for same
-Moses Hurt 1 day for same

PAGE 172

-Gilliam vs Newman, dismd

COURT Friday 27 October 1797 present: William Banks, Abraham Penn, James Lyon, Joseph Stovall, George Penn, Brett Stovall

-Reubin Banks vs William Banks executor of Gerrard Banks dec'd,Court of the opinion that the said Complaintant recover against the Defendant the negro girl Grace mentioned in the Bill together with her increase.
-Blankenship vs Chitwood, jury sworn: Edward Lewis, William Ross, William Goldson, James Taylor, Barnard Price, Jesse Reynolds, Richard Thomas, David Keaton, David Taylor, George Clark, James Finney, Samuel Clark Jr...verdict for Pltf.
-Morgan vs Breden, 2 suits
-Donalds executors vs Buford andothers..the Defendants, James Buford Sr and John Buford Jr not having entered their appearance or given security agreeable to the Act of Assembly and the rules of this Court and it appearing to the satisfaction of the Court that they are not inhabitants of this State..Said Bufords to appear in Court February next.
-Benjamin Phipott and Benjamin Goldson are appointed to view the stocks and report.

PAGE 173

-Elisha Blankenship is allowed 2 days and 50 miles coming and returning as witness for Blankenship vs Chitwood
-Walters vs Ogle, dismd
-A report of the view of the stocks was returned
-Jones vs Lewis
-Turman vs Kimzey, jury sworn: Moses Reynolds, Humphrey Smith, Henry Smith, George Clark, Joel Chitwood, William Lockart, Robert Hall, Richard Thomas, Joseph Keaton, William Ross, Joseph Going, Samuel Helton....verdict for Pltf in the amount of 15 pounds.
-John Allen and Thomas Allen vs Staples & Co, judgement
-Parr Jr vs Yeates
-Smith vs Lyon, contd, Joshua Rentfro and David Rogers Spl Bl
-Harris vs McPeak
-Commings vs Going
-William McPeak 2 days witness Turman vs Kimzey
-William McAlexander 2 days for same
-Ezekiel Morris 2 days for same-
-William Lockhart 2 days for same
-Saunders vs Henry & Morris
-Hanby vs Francis and others, on a motion of Complaintant, ordered thgt Isaac and Joseph Pennington be made Defendants in this suit.
-Moses Reynolds 1 day witness Cummings vs Goings
-Jesse Reynolds 1 day for same
-Biscoe assignee vs Smith, dismd
-Harvey Fitzgerald 1 day witness Cummings vs Goings
-John Dalton is recommended as 2nd Lt of Artillery in the place of W. Lindsay.
-David Rogers 2 days witness Gilliam vs Newman
-Wilson & Son vs Penn, A. Hughes security for costs.

PAGE 174

COURT Thursday 30 November 1797 present: Joshua Rentfro, Hamon Critz, Samuel Packwood, Brett Stovall, James Lyon.

-Deed- John Dempsey to George Hairston

PAGE 174 contd

-Deed- William Lindsay to George Hairston
-Gabriel Penn and John Hughes came into Court and produced commissions appointing them Justices of the Peace.
-Deed- John Lee to Brett Stovall
-Samuel Staples is recommended as a fit and proper person to serve as Major of the 1st Btn of Militia in place of Stephen Lyon who hath resigned.
-Penn vs Lindsay, on an atta. Jacob Michaux a garnishee served saith he owes the Defendant nothing.
-Samuel Clark, Gentleman, produced a Commission appointing him Sheriff of this County. Gabriel Penn, Samuel Clark Jr, George Clark appeared in Court and qualified as Deputy Sheriffs.
-Ordered the Overseers of the Poor bind out Abigail Burress to Laughlin Fagin..the child aged 6 years October last.
-Martin Dunkin Sr is exempt from the payment of County and Parish levies for the future.
-On a motion of Joel Chitwood an Injunction against him by Isham Blankenship..to stay the proceedings..security James Nolen.
-Biscoe assignee vs McCain
-same vs Haile

PAGE 175

-Commonwealth vs Surveyors of the Road from the top of Bull Mtn to John Turners, dismd.
-On a motion of Joseph Going for an Injunction to stay the proceedings of a Judgement of Joseph Keaton,...granted with Brett Stovall his security.
COURT adjourned until tomorrow.

COURT Thursday 25 January 1798 present: Joseph Stovall, Hamon Critz, Joshua Rentfro, John Hughes.

-William James Mayo, John Hancock, James Morris, Samuel Layne or any three to view a way to turn the road leading from Sycamore Creek to the Patrick Courthouse.
-Deed- David Morgan, Benjamin Kimzey andEzekiel Morris to William Turman, acknowledged by Morgan and one witness.
-Deed- James Denny, John Henry Sr and David Roberson to David Morgan.
-Deed- David Morgan to William Roberson
-Deed- James Lyon and William Mitchell to George Hairston and Joshua Rentfro.

PAGE 176

-Edward Lewis, an invalid pensioner of this State, came into Court and the Court is of the opinion that his pension should be continued.

County of Patrick for year 1797

to Sheriff, annual salary	25.
to Clerk for same and add for 6 months	37.50
to States Attorney	25.
to James Thompson for timber	1.62
to Clerk for services to the Commissioners	40.
to Sheriff for record book for the Clerk	8.
to Depositium for use of County	50.
to Sheriff for collecting 187 12 cents	11.22
	198.34

By 805 tithables @ 24 cents per poll

-Hall vs Harris
-Edward Tatum, Joshua Rentfro, Gabriel Penn or any two of them are appointed to settle with the former Sheriff for the depositium in their hands.
-John Dalton appeared in Court and qualified as a Collector to collect the acreages of taxes and Officers fees due Jonathan Hanby, late Sheriff of this County.

Page 176 contd

-Deed- John Lee to Brett Stovall

PAGE 177

COURT Thursday 22 February 1798 present: Brett Stovall, William Banks, Joseph Stovall, John Hughes.

-Power of attorney of Jacob Lindsay to Jacob Michaux
-Lease from Jonathan Hanby to James Taylor
-Rowan & Scott vs Frans, Samuel Clark Spl Bl
-Henry for the benefit of Denny vs Tuggle, dismd
-Saunders vs Harper, dismd
-Lackey vs Mayo, dismd
-James Taylor foreman, John Hoff, Samuel Harris, William McAlexander, Thomas Hollandsworth, Thomas Mitchell, John Medley Jr, Clement Rogers, George Rogers, James Ferrell, David Morgan, Christopher Long, Edward Lewis to serve as a Grand Jury for this County.
-Keaton vs Haile, dismd
-Overseers of the Poor to bind out James Sleator to William Brewer.
-Deed- Stephen Lyon, Sr, James Lyon Jr and William Mitchell to George Hairston and Joshua Rentfro.
-Rowan & Scott vs Hoff
-Rowan & Scott vs Corn
-Joyce vs Lyon and Lindsay
-Pursuant to an Act of Assembly in that case made, ordered that the Sheriff do only advertise that there will be an election held at the house of John Koger on the 1st Saturday in April next for the Overseer of the Poor for the district north of the Bull Mountain; also at Charles Fosters and the Sheriff do advertise an election for the lower district

PAGE 178
held at Josias Farris on the same day and Abraham Penn do superintend same. And there will be another election for the upper district held at the house where Rhoda Moore formerly lived with William Carter to superintend.

-Deed- Robert Rowan and Robert Scott to John Hughes
-Deed- Benjamin Yeates and wife to John Fry
-Rowan & Scott vs Critz
-Deed- Humphrey Posey to William King, further proved
-Leave is granted Jacob Michaux to keep an Ordinary at his house in the County with George Penn his security.
-Deed- John Dempsey to George Hairston
-Power of attorney of John Watin (Watson??) Sr to Samuel Staples and William Carter.
-John Cammeron is exempt from the payment of County and Parish levies for the future
-Penn vs Lindsay, George Penn a garnishee
-Jesse Corn qualified as Major of the Militia
Present: George Penn, Joshua Rentfro, Charles Foster..absent: Brett Stovall, Joseph Stovall and John Hughes.
-Richard Welch is exempt from the payment of County and Parish levies for the future.
-Ignatious Redman the same
-John Hollandsworth the same
-Rowan & Scott vs Ferrell
-Biscoe assignee vs Hall
-Moses Reynolds 1 day witness Commings vs Going

PAGE 179

COURT Thursday 23 February 1798 present: Stephen Lyon, Charles Foster, William Banks, John Hughes, George Penn, William Carter.

-Gilliam vs Newman
-Jones vs Lewis

Page 179 contd

-Jones executors vs Lewis
-Morgan vs Breden
-Parr vs Yeates, jury sworn: William Gholson, Arch. Hughes, Harvey Fitzgerald, Joseph Keaton, David Rogers, Robert Sharp, Joseph Reynolds, William Moore, Thomas Ellyson, Samuel Crutcher, John Medley Sr, Richard Pilson..a juror withdrew and continued.
-Deed- Isaac Hollandsworth and wife to Zachariah King
-Morgan vs Breden Jr, take deposition of James Lackey
-The present Sheriff wishes to continue in the office of Sheriff as long as the Law will admit him.
-Smith vs Lyon
-Harris vs McPeak
-Smith vs Taylor
-Power of attorney of Brett Stovall to John Allen
-Cummings vs Going, jury sworn: Richard Thomas, Harvey Fitzgerald, David Rogers, David Morgan, William Moore, Robert Sharp, Thomas Ellyson, Joseph Reynolds, John Medley Sr, Richard Pilson, John Sharp Jr, Archibald Shelton..verdict returned for the Defdt.
-Samuel Clark, gentleman sheriff, appeared in Court with Edward Tatum, Samuel Staples, William Banks, John Dalton, George Rogers and George Penn as his securities.
-James Lyon 1 day witness Newman vs Gilliam
-also two days witness Henry Smith vs Stephen Lyon

PAGE 180

-Jesse Reynolds 2 days witness Commings vs Going
-Richard Thomas 2 days for same
-Archibald Shelton 2 days for same
-Susannah Sharp 2 days for same
-Moses Reynolds 2 days for same
-Soloman Keaton 2 days for same and 2 days for John Parr Sr vs George Yeates
-Susannah Cockram 1 day witness Going vs Cummings
-Hughes assignee vs Lindsay, jury sworn: David Rogers, William Fitzgerald, Joseph Keaton, Samuel Harris, Moses Reynolds, Pleasant C. Reynolds, James Taylor, James Boyd, John Talbott, John Mankin, John Wilson...a juror withdrew and continued.
-David Morgan vs John Breden Jr
-White vs Tatum
-Pyrtle vs McNanney
-Boyd vs Carlin
-Douglas vs Carlin
-Douglas vs Adkinson
-Penington vs Bolling
-John Medley Jr 3 days witness Going vs Commings
-David Rogers 2 days witness Gilliam vs Newman
-William Adams 3 days witness Going vs Commings
-Isaac Dodson 1 day for same
-William Salsberry 1 day witness Morgan vs Breden
-Henry Smith 1 day witness Gilliam vs Newman
-Baird vs Reynolds & Smith, Edward Lewis Spl Bl
-Deed- Anthony Smith and Agathey Smith his wife to Sackville Brewer Jr together with a certificate of the Clerk of Hawkins Co TN where the said wife relinquished her right of dower.
-Jonathan Hanby, late sheriff, resumed his seat as a Justice.
-Harvey Fitzgerald 2 days witness Going vs Commings

PAGE 181

COURT Thursday 29 March 1798 present: Joshua Rentfro, William Carter, Brett Stovall, Daniel Carlin, Charles Foster, John Hughes.

-Deed- Garland Akin to John Redd
-Deed- Blizard Magruder to William Banks
-Deed- John Harvie, Richard Adams, William Duvall, trustees of Patrick Couts to Hamon Critz.

Page 181 contd

-Deed- John Harvie, Richard Adams, William Duvall, trustees of Patrick Couts to Jacob Farris
-Deed- Luke Foley to John Burnett
-Deed- John Redd to Thomas White Ruble
-Deed of Trust- Thomas W. Ruble to John Redd
-Deed- William Nowlin to James Pemberton
-Ordered that the road from William Perkins to the Main Road that leads to Peter Saunders at the top of the Hill at Shooting Creek be continued and kept in repair by William Perkins.
-Deed- Rachel Martindill, Daniel Martindill, John Martindill, Joseph Pennington and Grace Pennington to Richard Davison.
-Lease of lands from William Wilson to James Nowlin and wife.
-Overseers of the Poor to bind out John Sleator age 10 years.
-On a motion of Jacob Hite and T. R. McGaughey, a license is granted them to retail goods, wares and merchandize.
-On a motion of David Dishang?? the same.
-Deed- Joseph Stovall to Richardson Herndon
-Deed- Anthony Smith and wife Agathy to George Hairston
-Deed- Laughlin Fagin from Aaron Rea and wife
-Deed- Abel Perigoy to William Perkins
-Penn vs Going

PAGE 182

This COURT doth set and rate the following liquors, diets, etc.. Breakfast 1/6; dinner 2/; supper 1/6; lodging 6d; corn and oats per gal 6d; sheave of oats 2d; foddar the same; continental rum 16/ per gal; West India 24/; peach brandy 12/; whiskey 10/.

-Overseers of the Poor bind out Shadrack Sloan to David Morgan.
-Deed- Richard Davidson and wife to Rachel Martindill, Daniel Martindill and John Martindill.
-Deed- Elisabeth Laurence to Humphrey Smith
-Deed- Obadiah Hudson to Thomas Hudson
-Deed- James Lyon Sr and Daniel Carlin to Joshua Rentfro
-James Turner is recommended as a fit person to serve as Captain in place of Jesse Corn; John Turner as Lt., and William James Mayo as Ensign.
-George Lackey as Capt; Thomas R. Hall as Lt; William Fuson as Ensign.
-John Tatum as Capt, John Wilson as Lt; Jackson Smith as Ensign.
-Deed- Thomas Hudson to William Going
-Administration of the estate of Peter Simmons dec'd is granted James L. Gains with securities William Carter and Joshua Rentfro.
-John Nunns, John Rea, John Tatum to appraise said estate.
-Deed- Martin Simms to Joshua Adams
-James L. Gains is appointed guardian to Peter Simmons
-Deed- George Dodson to John Spencer
-Isaac Dodson not having appeared to his recognizance entered into, thou solemnly called and came not, it is considered by the Court that he has forfited the said recognizence; therefore, ordered by the Court that the Commonwealth do prosecute a suite against him.

PAGE 183

- Ordered that the Sheriff pay William Hannah $1.38 for overpayment in levies.
-Morgan vs Farrell, dismd
-Hairston vs Devonshire
-Robert Scott 1 day witness Penn vs Going
-Boyd vs Yoes, dismd
-Biscoe assignee vs Frans
-Peter Hairston vs Michaux
-Staples & Co for the benefit of John Dalton vs Wiatt Shelton
-Pennington vs Bolling
-Parsley assignee vs Coomer
-Sutton for the benefit of Gholson vs Carlin
-Lyon vs Newman

Page 183 contd

-Rowan & Scott vs Dodson

PAGE 184

COURT Thursday 26 April 1798 present: Charles Foster, Francis Turner, Jonathan Hanby, John Hughes, Stephen Lyon.

-Deed- Bartlett Reynolds to John Gray, further proved
-Deed- Hiram Wills to Stephen Jones
-Deed- Stephen Jones to Hiram Wills
-Deed- David Tittle to Benjamin Haile
-Deed- Charles Rakes to James Pemberton
-Deed- Martin Amos to Archer Barnard
-Deed- Stanwix Hord to Samson Jones
-Deed- J. Saunders to Nathan Morris
-Deed- Aron William to E. Deheart
-Deed- Thomas Plaster to Thomas Tenison
-Deed- Peter Bellow to Eli Bellow
-Deed- Peter Bellow to Elisha Bellow
-Deed- Peter Bellow to Elijah Bellow
-Deed- William Allen to Stephen Jones

-Augustine Thomas foreman, William Gray, John Turner, Isham Cradock, Beveridge Hughes, Nathaniel Ross, Richard Thomas, William Cloud, Spencer Talley, Joseph Johnson, John Medley Jr. William Allen, David Tittle, Thomas Mitchell, Hiram Wills, Moses Godward to serve as Grand Jury.

-Deed- Warsham Easley and William Easley to James L. Gains
-Deed- Abraham Mayse and William Witt to Zachariah King
-Deed- Joel Chitwood to John Pigg
-Deed- Abraham Mayse to Thomas Hollandsworth
-Deed- William Hickinbottom to Richard Adkinson
-Deed- Samuel Layne to Isham Burnett
-Deed- William Burnett to John Conner
-Deed- William McPeak to Samuel Harris
-Deed- William McPeak to James Thomson
-Deed- Jonathan Hanby to David Hanby
-Deed- William Gardner to William Branham Sr

PAGE 185

-Deed- William Cloud to William Collings
-Deed- Benjamin Yeates to John Fry, further proved
-Deed- John Lee to Edmond Brammer
-Deed- Thomas P. Jordon and wife to Peter Saunders, 2 deeds
-Deed- David Morgan, Benjamin Kimzey and Ezekiel Morris to William Turman, further proved
-Deed- Spencer Talley to Martin Talley
-Deed- Edward Tatum to William Tatum
-Deed of Gift - Isham Webb and wife to Spencer Talley
-Deed- James Denny, John Henry, David Robertson to David Morgan further proved
-Deed- Brett Stovall to William Hannah

PAGE 186

COURT Friday 27 April 1798 present: Francis Turner, Joshua Rentfro, Charles Foster, Hamon Critz, Abraham Penn, George Penn.

-Deed- Isham Webb and wife to William Webb and Isham Webb Jr
-Hall vs Dunkin & Fletcher, dismissed as to Fletcher the Defendant, John Dunkin not appearing and giving security and it appearing to the Court that he is not a resident of this State, ordered that he do appear at Court the last Thursday in July. Advertisement to made in the Virginia Gazette.

Page 186 contd

-Turman vs Kimzey
-Deed- William Harris to William Thorpe's heirs
-Dickson vs Gholson, Gabriel Penn Special Bail, and delivered the Defendant up and Joshua Rentfro and Henry Smith further Spl Bl.
-Carlin vs Wallace, Scott and others, Samuel Clark Jr, Special Bail delivered defendant up and John Hughes further Spl Bl.
-Commonwealth vs John Henry, judgement 83¢ and costs.
-Thomas B. Jones vs E. Lewis, jury sworn: William Fuson, William McAlexander, George Lackey, Samuel Harris, James Harris, William Frazier, James Elkins, Joel Chitwood, John Hall, John Eaden, Jesse Corn, David Ross.. verdict returned fro the Pltf for debt in the declaration and one penny damages.
-same exors vs same,..same jury..verdict for Pltf for costs
-Morgan vs Breden, 2 suits, contd
-Breden vs Morgan

PAGE 187

-Deed- Rachel Martindill, Daniel Martindill, John Martindill, Joseph and Grace Penington to Richard Davidson, further proved.
-Deed- Edmond Chitwood to George Penn and Samuel Staples
-Deed- John Chitwood to George Penn and Samuel Staples
-Deed- Susanah Camron to William Heath
-Deed- John Sharp Sr to Robert Sharp
-A release or relinquishment from John Lee to Thomas Ward
-William Moore qualified as Captain of Militia
-Samuel Clark,gentleman sheriff, appeared and objected to the sufficiency of the Jail.
-Abraham Penn, Charles Foster and William Carter the three gentlemen appointed to superintend the elections for Overseer of the Poor returned with their reports to wit: Lower District, James Taylor, Peter Frans and Brett Stovall were elected; District North of Bull Mountain, John Hall, William Packwood and Alexander Lackey were elected; Upper District, John Nunns, George Carter and Peter Bellow were elected.

-Gilliam vs Newman, jury sworn: James Harris, David Harbour, Richard Thomas, Peter Frans, Robert Sharp, Nathan Morrison, Joseph Going, Nathaniel Ross, Alexander Lackey, John Turman, Thomas Hornsby, Daniel Adams..a juror withdrew and continued.

-Deed- Misheck Perdue to James Ferrell further proved
-Deed- Anthony Tittle and wife to George Hairston, further proved
-Harris vs McPeak, defendant appeared and acknowledged that the Pltf was not guilty of the charge in the declaration..fined $20.00 and cost.
-Lewis vs Eckolds for reasons appearing to the Court, sent back to the Rules.
-Nathaniel Helton 2 days witness Harris vs McPeak
-Deed- Blizard Magruder to William Banks, further proved
-Joseph Reynolds 2 days witness Harris vs McPeak
-Smith vs Tenison

PAGE 188

-Harris vs Shelton, Samuel Duvall, Spl Bl, 2 suits
-Parr vs Yeates, jury sworn: David Ross, Samuel Harris, Joseph Koger, Joseph Newman, George Carter, Lewis Foster, John Chapman, John Mankin, Edward Lewis, James Carlin, William Burnett, Isham Cradock..verdict for Pltf amount $293.00.

-James Taylor, Peter Frans, George Carter, John Hall and Alexander Lackey qualified as Overseers of the Poor.
-Boyd vs Carlin, dismd

Page 188 contd

-Smith vs Lyon, jury sworn: David Ross, Samuel Harris, Joseph Koger, George Fulcher, Laughlin Fagan, Lewis Foster, John Chapman, John Mankin, Edward Lewis, James Carlin, William Burnett, Isham Cradock, ..a juror withdrew and continued.
-William Lyon 1 day witness Newman vs Gilliam
-James Lyon same
-Gilliam vs Newman referred to Joshua Rentfro, Edward Tatum, Samuel Staples.
-Soloman Keaton 1 day witness Parr vs Yeates
-Sarah Ogle 1 day witness Lyon vs Smith
-Eliphaz Shelton 1 day witness Lyon vs Smith
-Jackson Smith 4days witness Gilliam vs Newman
-John Ogle 1 day witness Lyon vs Smith
-Rowan & Scott vs Mayo, Alexander Lackey Spl Bl
-Samuel Staples & Co vs Mayo, Alexander Lackey Spl Bl
-William Burnett 1 day witness John Breden vs Morgan
-Elihu Ayres 1 day witness Lyon vs Smith
-William Reynolds 1 day for same
-William James Mayo 1 day witness J. Breden vs Morgan
-William Salsbury same
-William Cloud 1 day witness Lyon vs Smith

PAGE 189

COURT Saturday 28 April 1798 present: Charles Foster, Charles Thomas, Francis Turner, Joshua Rentfro.

-Penn vs Penn, dismd
-Lindsay for the benefit of Michaux vs Penn
-White vs Tatum
-Call vs Studham, Judgement amount of $10.00
-Commonwealth vs Breden Jr.
-Hughes assignee vs Lindsay, jury sworn: David Taylor, George Lackey, George Rogers, Joshua Adams, Richard Thomas, James Carlin, George Corn, Nathaniel Ross, David Ross, Lewis Foster, David Rogers, George Fulcher ..verdict for Pltf £80.

-Pyrtle vs McNanney, dismd
-Hanby vs Marrs representatives
-Ellison vs same
-Hairston vs same
-Penington vs same
-Harris vs same
-Susannah Marr, widow and relict of John Marr dec'd, is appointed guardian to defend the orphans of said decedent in these suits.
-Douglas vs Adkinson, contd
-Baird vs Reynolds
-Breden Jr vs Morgan, deposition of Thomas Goodson Jr to be taken.
-Smith vs Vest
-J. Hanby vs Joseph Francis, John Mankin, Susannah Marr widow and relict of John Marr dec'd, George Lent Washington Marr, John Marr, William Miller Marr, Sally Marr, Constant Harden Marr, Peter Nicholas Marr, Anna alias Agness Marr children of and heirs of John Marr dec'd. The Defendant Joseph Francis not having entered his appearance and not an inhabitant of this State...to appear last Thursday in July.
-Pennington vs same

PAGE 190

-Clark vs Koger, jury sworn: John Hanby, William Tatum, James Carlin, William Martin, Nathaniel Smith, Harvey Fitzgerald, George Rogers, David Rogers, John Mankin, William Lawson, Joseph Curd, William Deal. Verdict for Defendant.

Page 190 contd

-Jemimah Sharp 2 days witness Koger vs Clark
-James Morrison same
-Jesse Corn same
-James Ferrell same
-William Frazier same
-Nathan Morrison same
-Elisabeth Koger same
-Lewis Foster same
-Joseph Koger 2 days witness and coming and returning 220 miles
-Charles Foster 2 days witness Koger vs Clark
-Richard Thomas same
-Thomas Mitchell same
-James Elkins same
-Isaac Dodson 1 day witness Koger vs Clark
-Joshua Adams 2 days for same
-Isaac Dodson allowed 1 day witness Gilliam vs Newman
-Charles Thomas 2 days witness for Koger vs Clark
-Staples vs Scott, referred to Edward Tatum and Francis Turner.
-Joseph Willis appointed Constable in place of Thomas R. Hall.
-Isaac Dodson appeared in Court with David Rogers his security being indebted to the Overseers of the Poor in the amount of Five pounds per annum for 5 years in case the County becomes chargeable for a bastard child said Dodson begot on the body of Jane Barton.
-Overseers of the Poor vs I. Dodson and N. Smith his security, he having complyed with the request of the Law in that case, therefore, same is dismissed.
-Moore vs Rogers, contd
-Going vs Keaton, contd

PAGE 191

COURT Thursday 31 May 1798 present: Hamon Critz, Brett Stovall, Francis Turner, Joshua Rentfro.

-Deed- Isham Webb and wife to William Webb and Isham Webb Jr, further proved.
-Deed- Isham Webb and wife to Spencer Talley, further proved
-Deed- Palmer Scritchfield to Spencer Talley, further proved
-Deed- Moses Hughes to Spencer James
-John Nunns and Brett Stovall qualified as Overseers of the Poor.
-Benjamin Philpott surveyor of the streets in the Town of Taylorsville, ordered that all the citizens of the Town be his gang.
-Harvey Fitzgerald appointed surveyor of the road from Patrick Courthouse to the top of the Bull Mountain in place of Joshua Adams.
-William James Mayo is appointed with his hands to clear and open the road viewed from John Turners to the top of the Bull Mountain.
-Charles Foster and John Koger are appointed to settle with Isham Cradock, the administrator of Samuel King deceased, accounts current of the said decedent, it having appeared to the Court that the charges of the said Administrator is unreasonable and ought to be expunged.
-Power of attorney of Woolman Studham to Samuel Staples and William Carter.
-Deed- George Yeates to Sary Yeates
-Staples & Co for benefit of Dalton vs Shelton, dismd
-Hairston vs Devenshire, contd
-Peter Hairston vs Michaux, contd
-Lyon Jr vs Newman, contd
-Howell vs Atkins, dismd
-Baker vs Yoes, contd
-Callaway vs Chitwood, Judgement
-Doyal vs Edward, contd
-Gholson vs Price, N.P.
-Shadrick Going is exempt from the payment of County and Parish levies for the future.
-On a motion of James Calaway for a Judgement vs John Tatum.

PAGE 192

-Dickson vs Gholson, Joshua Rentfro and Henry Smith Spl Bl, delivered up the said Defendant whereupon he is prayed into custody, Samuel Staples and Joshua Rentfro further Special Bail.

COURT Thursday 28 June 1798 present: William Carter, Charles Foster, Edward Tatum, Joshua Rentfro.

-Deed- Martin Dickerson to Stephen Sisney
-Deed- William Amos to Martin Amos
-Deed- Jesse Corn to Mary Amos
-Deed- Elijah Dehart to Gabriel Dehart
-Deed- Rhoda Moore to William Moore
-Deed- Cornelius Keith to Nathaniel Stewart, 2 deeds
-Deed- Daniel Carlin to Abraham Hawks
-Deed- Nathaniel Stewart to William Perkins
-Deed- Abraham Penn to George Hairston
-Deed- Nathaniel Stewart to William Perkins

-On a motion of George Ashworth, admit him to build a water grist mill on Lovings Creek being the owner on both sides of said Creek.
-Deed- John Koger to George Hairston
-Hairston vs Devonshire, contd
-P. Hairston vs Michaux, contd
-Lyon Jr vs Newman, contd
-Baker vs Yoes, contd
-Doyal vs Edwards, contd at Defendants cost
-Deed- Samuel Perry and wife to Joseph Miller
-Martin Dickerson 1 day and 67 miles witness John Edwards vs Martin Doyal.
-Deed- Joseph R. Johnson to William Carter
-Deed- Joseph R. Johnson to George Ashworth

PAGE 193

-Jeremiah Jadwin is appointed surveyor of the road from the Carolina line to the top of the mountain at the Flower Gap.
-Parr Sr assignee vs Hawkins, Judgement $9.00 and cost.
-Joseph Keaton a garnishee being served saith he has in his possession 1 loom, 1 cotton and flax Wheel, 2 pots, 2 pales, 1 churn and 2 shoots of the Defendants effects.
-Going vs Findley, contd
-Breden Jr vs Morga, deposition of Isbell Dickerson to be taken.
-Breden Jr vs Commonwealth
-Deed- Jonathan Jennings and William Carter to David Hanby Sr, acknowledged as to Carter and acknowledged before two magistrates as to Jennings by the Clerk of Oglethorpe, Georgia.
-Deed- George Carter to William Carter
-On a motion of Edward Lewis to stay a Judgement against him by Thomas B. Jones executors..granted with Humphrey Smith his security.
-Harbour vs Corn, deposition of Martin Amos to be taken.

PAGE 194

COURT Thursday 26 July 1798 present: Joseph Stovall, Brett Stovall, George Penn, Edward Tatum, Joshua Rentfro, William Banks.

-Last Will and Testament of Richard Tucker Maynor dec'd exhibited by Ann Maynor and son Stephen Mayor as Administrators with security John Philpott and Joseph Cummings.
-Richard Stone, Joseph Cummings, John Medley Sr, Ignatious Sims are to appraise said estate.
-Ordered that the appointment of James L. Gains as Administrator of Peter Simmons dec'd be null and void.
-Coleman vs Marler, referred to Brett Stovall and Peter Frans.

Page 194 contd

-Archelaus Hughes foreman, Jesse Corn, Beveridge Hughes, John Hall, James Morrison, Moses Harbour, Clifton Keaton, William McAlexander, James McBride, Reubin Harris, Robert Lockhart, Samuel Layne, William Burnett, Richard Stone, James Bartlett, David Taylor to serve as Grand Jury.

Present: Hamon Critz, Francis Turner, Jonathan Hanby, John Hughes.
-Peter Scales recommended as a proper person to serve as Commissioner of the Peace.
-Samuel Clark, William Carter, Stephen Lyon recommended as -------
-Absent: Stephen Lyon, Brett Stovall, John Hughes, Edward Tatum, Jonathan Hanby, Charles Thomas, Joshua Rentfro.
-Patt, a negro wench belonging to Isaac Adams is exempt from the payment of levies during her inability.

PAGE 195

-Carlin	vs	Wallace and others	dismd
-Breden	vs	Turman	"
-Chandler	vs	McCain	"
-Rickman	vs	Koger	"
-Ross	vs	Keaton	"
-Hanby	vs	Hughes	"
-Jones	vs	Martin and wife	"
-Cross	vs	Gholson	"

-Commonwealth vs sundries on presentments made at February and April Courts are dismissed as some of the Jurors being illegal.
-West vs Gholson, Gabriel Penn, Arch. Hughes and John Dalton, Spl Bl.

COURT Friday 27 July 1798 present: Stephen Lyon, Brett Stovall, William Carter, George Penn.

-Hall vs Dunkin..Defendant not appearing ordered that the fee simple title in the land and premius in the deed exhibited be vested to said Complainant.
-Hairston vs Shelton, Judgement
-Rowan & Scott vs May, plea waved, Judgement confessed according to specialty and cost reserving equity
-Hairston vs Shelton, Judgement
-Staples & Co for G. Penn vs Mayo, Judgement
-Deed- Sarah Harris, James Harris, Henry Harris, Lucy Harris, Elisabeth Harris, William Harris, Rubin Harris to James Harris further proved.

PAGE 196

-Douglas	vs	Atkinson	contd
-White	vs	Tatum	"

-Moore vs Rogers, jury sworn: John Huff, William Creasey, Samuel Henry, William Roberson, Elisha Blankenship, Samuel Harris, Joseph Going, John Turner, Rueben Harris, Thomas Tenison, Henry Thompson, verdict for Pltf in the amount of $100.
-Deed- George Penn, Brett Stovall to Henry L. Briscoe
-Smith vs Poteet and others, for reasons appearing to the Court, this case is remanded to September Court.

-Staples & Co	vs	Booth	contd
-Going	vs	Keaton	"
-Dodson	vs	Scott	dismd
-Gray	vs	Thomas	not guilty

-Dickson vs Gholson, Samuel Staples and Joshua Rentfro Spl Bl
-West vs Gholson, Gabriel Penn, John Dalton, Archelaus Hughes are Special Bail.
-Smith vs Lyon, it appearing from a copy of a Judgement produced from the District Court that the Plaintiff recovered his costs on the----- to remove the cause from this Court to the District Court, therefore it is considered by the Court that the Plaintiff recover against the Defendant his costs by him expended in his defense in the original suit in this Court.

Page 196 contd

-John Newman allowed 2 days witness Moore vs Rogers
-Morgan vs Breden, jury sworn: Zachariah Keaton, Robert Sharp, John Huff, George Fulcher, Elijah Dehart, William Creasey, Thomas Tenison, Elihu Ayrs, Eliphaz Shelton, David Rogers, Clifton Keaton, William Keaton..verdict returned for Pltf.
-Breden vs Morgan..same jury as above..verdict of L28.6.9 damages for Plaintiff.

PAGE 197

-Smith vs Lyon, jury sworn: William Sharp, George Lackey, George Corn, Moses Reynolds, James Taylor, William McPeak, Henry Thompson, William Rogers, Isaac Breden, Jeremiah Burnett Jr, John Newman and Reubin Harris..verdict for Pltf L23.2.4.
-Elijah Dehart 1 day witness Smith vs Vest
-Coleman vs Marler, plaintiff to pay all cost
-William Burnett 2 days witness David Morgan vs J. Breden
-William Roberson 2 days for same
-David Dickerson 2 days and 50 miles for same
-Breden Jr vs Morgan, each party to take deposition on giving the adverse party legal notice.
-Dickson vs Gholson
-West vs Gholson
-David Harbour allowed 2 days witness Morgan vs Breden
-Lyon vs Smith, David Rogers his security
-Penington vs Hanby and others
-William McPeak 1 day witness Morgan vs Breden
-Morgan vs Breden, jury sworn: John Ogle, William Keaton, John Medley Jr, Frederick Fitzgerald, George Fulcher, Robert Sharp, David Rogers, Stephen Smith, John Huff, Samuel Harris, James Lyon, John Bennett. Verdict returned for Pltf L20.9.4.
-Staples & Co for benefit of John Hughes vs Dalton, George Lackey Special Bail.
-Eliphaz Shelton 1 day witness Smith vs Lyon
-William Sharp 1 day witness Clark vs Breden
-John Henry Sr 2 days witness A. Breden vs Morgan
-Lewis vs Stone, dismd
-Breden vs Morgan, referred to the Court and their judgement to be final..Court of the opinion the Defendant recover Judgement for his costs.

PAGE 198

-Samuel Henry 2 days 27 miles witness Morgan vs Breden
-Jeremiah Burnett Jr 2 days witness Breden vs Clark
-Joseph Reynolds 2 days witness John Breden Jr vs Commonwealth, also 1 day A. Breden vs Samuel Clark
-Samuel Harris 2 days witness Morgan vs A. Breden
-Henry Thompson 1 day for same
-Henry Thompson 1 day witness Morgan vs J. Breden
-Smith vs Lyon..David Rogers, Joshua Rentfro Special Bail
-Drury Bundren allowed 2 days witness Breden vs Clark
-Gabriel Penn allowed 6/ for services rendered in removing Halls property.

COURT Saturday 28 July 1798 present: Stephen Lyon, Francis Turner, Brett Stovall, John Hughes.

-Chitwood vs Blankenship
-Going vs Chitwood, referred to Brett Stovall, Gabriel Penn, John Hughes.
-Douglas vs Adkinson
-Breden vs Clark, jury sworn: David Rogers, Pleasant C. Reynolds, George Rogers Jr, William Rogers, William Parr, David Taylor, Henry Smith, Samuel Harris, James Taylor, Robert Rogers, Robert Sharp, Richard Davidson..verdict returned for Defendant.

Page 198 contd

-Deed- Martin Sims to Joshua Adams, further proved
-Joseph Reynolds 1 day witness Breden vs Clark
-Joseph Breden 2 days for same
-Drury Bundren 1 day for same
-Reubin Harris 2 days for same

PAGE 199

-James Harris 2 days witness Breden vs Clark
-Alexander Lackey same
-Francis Turner same
-James Turner same
-Adam Turner same
-William Sharp 1 day for same
-John Turner 2 days for same
-Coroner returned into Court his list of taxable property for the year 1798 and qualified same.

COURT Thursday 30 August 1798 present: Francis Turner, Brett Stovall, Joseph Stovall, Edward Tatum.

-James Sublett is exempt from the payment of County and Parish levies for the future.
-Thomas Collings the same
-Peter Bellow appointed surveyor of the road from Roda Moores old place to Little Dan River in place of Roda Moore.
-Ordered that John Turner, William Burnett, William Salsberry, John Davenport, Malichi Branham, David Branham, Obadiah Burnett, John Gardner, William Gardner, William Branham, Charles Scott and James Bolling be added to William James Mayos list of hands.
-Deed- Peter Hale and wife to Soloman Jones
-Deed- Benjamin Kimzey to George Booth
-Peter Bellow qualified as Overseer of the Poor
-Hairston vs Devonshire contd
-Peter Hairston vs Michaux contd
-Lyon Jr vs Newman, Judgement 56/6.
-Archer vs Corn dismd
-Baker vs Yoes, Judgement 3.13.0
-Doyal vs Edwards, Court of the opinion the Defendant recover Judgement for his costs
-Hughes Administrators vs McCain dismd

PAGE 200

-Samuel Clark Jr, Deputy Sheriff, returned into Court three lists of insolvents, one for land, one of negros and horses and the other tithes each for the year 1797.
-A relinquishment or quit claim from Elinor Foley co-heir of Bartlett Foley dec'd to H. Smith
-Hughes vs Hanby dismd
-James Boyd 1 day witness Edwards vs Doyal
-John Johnson 1 day for same
-Reubin Payne 1 day witness and 28 miles Martin Doyal vs John Edwards
-Woodson Hammond recommended as Ensign of Militia in the place of Mitchell Thompson of the 2nd Btn.
-Bill of Sale- Elisa Lawson to Edward Tatum
-Breden vs Tuggle contd
-Hughes vs Philpott Judgement
-Going vs Findley dismd
-Deed- Abraham Penn to George Hairston, further proved
-Edward Tatum, Commissioner of the County, allowed $80. for his services rendered for present year.
-On a motion of Zachariah Keaton for an injunction to stay the proceedings of a Judgement obtained against him by William Lindsay assignee for George Hairston....granted with William Keaton his security.
-Going vs Keaton, Referees discharged
-John Hanby allowed 1 day witness Philpott vs Hughes

PAGE 201

COURT 27 September 1798 present: Edward Tatum, Samuel Packwood, Abraham Penn, Joshua Rentfro.

-Deed- John Redd to Ignatious Simms
-Deed- Moses Hughes to Spencer James, further proved
-William Packwood qualified as Overseer of the Poor
-Deed- William Gilliam to Terry Hughes
-Deed- Adam Tittle and wife to George Hairston
-Letice Hagins appeared in Court and craved the peace of Nathan Morrison, whereupon said Morrison appeared in Court with David Harbour and James Turner his security to be of good behavior 12months 1 day.
-William Hanner appointed surveyor of the road in place of John Frans from Magruders Cabin to the ford of Spoon Creek above Hamon Critz.
-Bartlett Smith, James Dickerson, John Creed, Thomas Whitlock or any three to view a way for a road from Paul Howells to Wards Gap.
-Breden vs Morgan, take deposition of B. Kimzey
-Breden vs Morgan take the deposition of James Lyon
-Elisha Collings appointed surveyor of the road from the Dry Pond to the Widow Easleys Prise Beam in place of John Wilson.
-Deed- Samuel Perry and wife to Joseph Miller, further proved.

PAGE 202

COURT Thursday 25 October 1798 present: Hamon Critz, John Hughes, Edward Tatum, Jonathan Hanby, William Carter, Joshua Rentfro and Peter Scales.

-Deed- Archelaus Hughes Sr to Archelaus Hughes, further proved
-Deed- Henry Smith to Terry Hughes, Margaret Smith wife of Henry Smith relinquishes her right of dower.
-Deed- James Doak and wife to Garrett Branson
-Deed- Micajah Burnett and wife to John Burnett
-Ann Taylor vs P. Boman, dismissed at Defendants cost
-Miller and wife vs P. Boman, same
-Breden vs Breden, dismd at Pltf cost
-Augustine Thomas foreman, Beveridge Hughes, Richard Pilson, James Morrison, James Turner, John Turner, David Taylor, John Hoff, Samuel Harris, John Conner, John Chitwood, Moses Harbour, Jeremiah Burnett Sr, Robert Lockhart, Adrian Anglin, James Fulkerson, Richard Thomas to serve as Grand Jury.
-Smith vs Brewer dismissed
-Peter Scales qualified as Justice of the Peace and Justice in Chancery.
-Webb vs Sutton, Eliphaz Shelton security for Plaintiff cost

County of Patrick for year 1798

Clerks annual salary	25.
Sheriffs annual salary	25.
Deputy States Attorney salary	25.
Garrett Gibson 8 young wolf heads	16.64
same for 7 young wolf heads	14.56
Aron Boweran 1 old wolf head	4.17
Eliphaz Shelton for hauling timer for a coaseway	1.70

-John Dalton appointed Commissioner of this County
-Laughlin Fagan appointed Constable in place of John Wilson.

PAGE 203

COURT 26 October 1798 present: Edward Tatum, Francis Turner, John Hughes, Peter Scales.

-Sheriff to pay Jeremiah Burnett Sr $1.16 for overcharge
-Lewis vs Eckolds, next term

Page 203 contd

-Penington vs Hanby and others, the Captain having made a deposit with the Clerk sufficient to pay all costs. I, Samuel Staples do bond myself to pay all cost that may arise in the case.
-Creasey vs Ayrs dismd
-Smith vs Poteet and others
-Gray vs Thomas dismd
-White vs Tatum contd
-Breden Jr vs Morgan contd
-Deed- Micajah Burnett and wife to John Burnett further proved
-Joshua Adams 1 day witness Tatum vs White
-Staples & Co vs Booth, jury sworn: John Huff, David Keaton, William Sublett, William Frazier, Richard Thomas, John Medley Jr, Barnard M. Price, Edward Lewis, Alexander Lackey, William Harrod, Frederick Fitzgerald, John Rea...Verdict returned for Pltf, the amount of the Bond.
-Lyon vs Smith
-Smith vs Tenison
-Ogle vs Walter, Gabriel Penn, Spl Bl
-Corn vs Harbour contd
-Morrison vs Harbour dismd
-Morrison vs Harbour and wife dismd
-Johnson vs Johnson contd
-Going vs Newman..take deposition of Francis Dolehite

PAGE 204

-Jacob Critz allowed 1 day witness Gray vs Thomas
-Hannah Mayo 2 days for same
-William Sublett 2 days for same
-James Fulkerson same
-John Ward same
-William Frazier 2 days witness Corn vs Harbour
-James Morrison same
-Benjamin Haile same
-Nathaniel Ross same
-Francis Dolahite 2 days witness John Going vs Joseph Newman
-Samuel Clark, gentleman sheriff, with Archelaus Hughes, John Hughes, Edward Tatum, Samuel Staples, Gabriel Penn his securities for the true and faithfull collecting revenues for 1798, Bond $30,000.

-Chitwood vs Blankenship contd
-Hairston vs Marrs heirs
-Hairston vs Marrs heirs, ordered that Thomas Hardman be appointed guardian in place of Susannah Hardman, formerly Susannah Marr, administratrix of John Marr dec'd.
-Gilliam vs Newman redocket
-Hugnes vs Philpott, Harvey Fitzgerald Special Bail

PAGE 205

COURT 29 November 1798 present: Brett Stovall, Jonathan Hanby, Hamon Critz, Peter Scales.

-Power of attorney of Joshua Adams to William Adams
-Overseers of the Poor bind out Robert King, orphan child.
-Also William Balile and Barnaba Balile orphans of Susanah Balile.
-Harris vs Marrs heirs..the Defendant George Lent Washington Marr not having entered his appearance and given security, not an inhabitant of this State..to appear the last Thursday in February next.
-Falkner and wife vs Soloman
-Deed- William Bristoe and wife to Richard Massey
-Deed- James Bolin to Gabriel Foley and Artermency Foley.
-Isaac Breden appointed Constable in place of William McPeak
-Parr vs Keaton Judgement

Page 205 contd

County levy for 1798 forward	112.07
Clerk for service to Commissioners	40.
Depositium for use of County	30.
Sheriff for collecting	10.
	192.07

By 988 tithes @ 19 cents per poll

-David Roberson Jr 1 day witness Breden vs Tuggle
-William Cherry appointed surveyor of the road from Mayo River near Francis old place to the Caroline line.
-James Taylor, John Camron, William Deal, Joel Chitwood or any three to view a way for a road from Ran..... Path to Renns Spring.

PAGE 206

COURT 31 January 1799 present: William Banks, Charles Thomas, Brett Stovall, Joseph Stovall.

-Deed- Daniel Carlin to Abram Hawks, further proved
-Deed- William Perkins to Thomas Carr
-Deed- Isham Pucket to John Yeates alias Smith
-Deed- John Smith alias Yeates to Thomas Summers
-Deed- Henry Lyne to Gabriel Penn
-Overseers of the Poor bind out James Innes Jr to Jacob Critz
-Last Will and Testament of Isham Webb, deceased, exhibited by his widow and relict, proved by witness. Letter of Administration granted Ann the said widow with surety: Martin Talley and Jeremiah Jadwin.
-William Cloud, James Dickerson, Jacob Johnson, Thomas Whitlock to appraise the said estate.
-Ordered that the hands contained in the list of Jeremiah Jadwin to be exempt from working on any other road.
-Deed- Blizard Magruder to William Banks
-Deed- Benjamin Garrett to William Garrett
-Inventory of the estate of Richard T. Maynor returned
-Hairston vs Devonshire contd
-Peter Hairston vs Michaux contd
-Breden vs Tuggle Judgement
-Adams vs Keaton contd
-David Roberson Jr 1 day witness Isaac Breden vs Tuggle
-Duvall vs Shelton Judgement
-Duvall vs Chitwood Judgement
-Duvall vs Smith contd
-Duvall vs Keaton contd
-Duvall vs Adkinson Judgement
-Reynolds vs Davis Judgement
-Smith vs Bates N.P.
-Bryan vs Perkins for benefit of Humphrey Smith, contd
-Hoff vs Peregoy
-Smith vs Bates

PAGE 207

-Banks vs Brewer Judgement
-Michaux vs Hughes contd
-John Miller 1 day witness Michaux vs Hughes
-Stovall vs Philpott
-Jessops exors vs Magruder
-Charles Thomas 1 day and 20 miles witness Perkins vs Bryan
-Charles Thomas Jr same
-Thomas R. Hall 1 day for same
-Edward Lewis, invalid pensioner appeared in Court..pension to be continued.
-Smith vs Laurence, Martin Amos Special Bail
-Deed- Jesse Corn to Matthew Moore
-John Dalton qualified as 2nd Lt of Artillery

PAGE 208

COURT 28 February 1799 present: Hamon Critz, Charles Foster, Joshua Rentfro, Edward Tatum.

-Deed- Owen Ruble to Jacob Stover
-Breden and wife vs Chandler and wife, John Bennett, Francis Nowlin, Joshua Adams, Samuel Staples, Daniel Adams are Special Bail.
-Deed- Samuel Clark Sr to William Mitchell

COURT 1 March 1799 present: Charles Foster, George Penn, Joshua Rentfro, Abraham Penn, Peter Scales.

-Penington vs Hanby and others
-Webb vs Sutton
-Johnson vs Johnson
-Smith vs Brewer dismd
-Biggs vs Ross dismd
-William James Mayo qualified as Ensign of Militia
-Breden vs Morgan contd
-White vs Morgan contd
-Joshua Adams 2 days witness Tatum vs White
-David Hanby same
-Gabriel Penn same
-Lyon vs Smith contd
-Ogle vs Walter contd
-Corn vs Harbour not guilty
-Newman vs Going, jury sworn: Claiborne Shelton, Francis Nowlin, David Morgan, Sharp Barton, Zachariah Keaton, Joel Chitwood, James Lyon, John Burnett, Thomas Hornsby, Alexander Lackey, James Lyon, David Harbour, Zachariah King..verdict for Pltf.
-Deed- Henry Lyne to Gabriel Penn, further Proved
-Deed- Abram(Abner) Eckolds to Jasiel Eckolds, Talman Harbour to pay.

PAGE 209

-James Morrison 2 days witness Corn vs Harbour
-David Tittle same
-Benjamin Hale same
-William Frazier same
-John Bolt 2 days 20 miles witness Corn vs Harbour
-Nathaniel Ross 2 days witness Corn vs Harbour
-Humphrey Smith same
-Charles Foster same
-Beasley vs Ellyson dismd
-Saunders vs Ross, Gabriel Penn, George Fulcher Spl Bl
-Trigg vs Reynolds, Peter Frans Spl Bl
-John Hill 2 days witness Newman vs Going
-John Witt 2 days 16 miles for same
-John Gossett 2 days for same
-Leave is granted Jacob Critz to keep an Ordinary at his house in the County with Samuel Clark Jr his security.
-Chitwood vs Blankenship contd
-Bolt vs Chandler and wife, William J. Mayo and Samuel Staples Spl Bl
-Jesse Tatum Sr 2 days witness Newman vs David Going
-Smith vs Poteet, to take depositions with notice

PAGE 210

COURT 28 March 1799 present: Charles Thomas, Joseph Stovall, John Hughes, Brett Stovall, Francis Turner.

-Deed- Micajah Burnett and wife to John Burnett, further proved
-Deed- William Adams to Sharp Barton..Sarah Adams wife of William Adams relinquishes her right of dower
-James Denny, Richard Pilson, William Sloan, William McAlexander or any three to view a way for a road from James Harris to James Dennys.
-Deed- Sharp Barton to John Fenny, Sarah Barton wife of Sharp Barton

Page 210 contd

relinquishes her right of dower.
-Power of attorney of Timothy Stamps to Charles Foster from under the hands of the Clerk of Elbert County, Georgia relative to the conveyance of lands.
-Adams Turner, Jeremiah Burnett Jr, Jeremiah Burnett Sr and William Pilson or any three to view a way for a road from Francis Turners to the Meeting House.
-On a motion of George Booth to stay the proceedings of a Judgement obtained against him by Staples and Company assignee of Breden granted with James Harris and Joseph Reynolds his security.
-Harbour vs Lewis Judgement
-Deed- Bartemus Reynolds and wife to John Adams
-Déed- David Rowark to Perry Green Johnson
-Deed- William Gardner to Jesse Corn
-On a motion of John Going for an injunction to stay the proceedings against him, granted with Jacob Adams and Adrian Anglin his security.
-Saunders vs Keaton Judgement
-George Hairston vs Devonshire contd
-Peter Hairston vs Michaux contd
-Adams vs Keaton contd
-David Going vs Edward Bolling dismd
-Duvall vs Keaton Judgement
-A Mortgage from William Mitchell to William Buckly, Treasurer of the Commonwealth..charge to William Mitchell and Thomas Mitchell.
-Deed of Trust- Joel Chitwood to George Penn

Present: Joseph Stovall, Joshua Rentfro, John Hughes,Hamon Critz

-Bryan for the benefit of H. Smith vs Perkins --dismd
-John Miller 1 day witness Michaux vs Hughes
-Smith vs Bates N.P.

PAGE 211

-Charles Thomas 1 day witness Bryant vs Wm. Perkins Sr
-Thomas R. Hall same
-Hugh Boyd same
-Charles Thomas Jr 1 day 20 miles for same
-Humphrey Smith 1 day same

-William Sharp, Jesse Corn, John Koger, George Lackey or any three to view a way for a road from the top of Bull Mountain across Blackberry Creek.

COURT 25 April 1799 present: Francis Turner, Brett Stovall, William Banks, William Carter.

-Deed- Abraham Penn to Webb Nash
-Deed- John Yeates to Jacob Talbott
-Deed- William Grigg to Jacob Talbott
-Deed- James Ingram to Abel Peregoy
-James Taylor foreman, James Morrison, Alexander Lackey, Jesse Corn, Nathaniel Ross, David Morgan, Humphrey Smith, George Penn Sr, Augustine Thomas, James Haile, William Frazier, Sharp Barton, David Taylor, Peter Frans, William Fitzgerald, John Adams to serve as Grand Jury.
-Wales?? vs Stone dismd
-Danger vs Taylor and others dismd
-White vs Tatum, take deposition of William Lyons Jr, James Martin, Charles Beasley, Joseph Cloud, Mat. Moore, John Martin are appointed Commissioner for that purpose or any three of them.
-Frans vs Banks, Samuel Staples Spl Bl
-Harris vs Critz, James Dickerson Spl Bl
-Ordered that David Keaton and his gang with Jacob Critz gang do repair the bridge over Spoon Creek.
-Lyon vs Smith contd
-Ogle vs Walter contd

Page 211 contd

-Trigg vs Reynolds, Peter Frans, Special Bail
-Deed- Job Ross to Cornelius Fonehand??
-Deed- John Burnett to Elisha Packwood
-Deed- William Dabney and wife to Daniel Askin

PAGE 212

-Deed- James Lyon Sr, James Lyon Jr and William Mitchell to George Hairston and Joshua Rentfro, further proved
-Stewart vs Carlin Judgement
-King vs Peterson, Augustine Thomas, Jacob Critz Spl Bl
-Trigg vs Reynolds, his Special Bail having delivered him up and being prayed into custody, whereupon Jonathan Hanby appeared in Court and entered further Special Bail for the Defendant.
-John Tatum vs Isaac Penington, Samuel Staples Spl Bl
-Deed- Isaac Penington to Samuel Staples
-Hairston vs Marrs heirs, on hearing said Bill, the Court do decree and order that the land and appertanances in said Bill be vested in the Complainants in fee simple and that the said George Lent Washington Marr, Constant Hardin Marr, John Marr, William Miller Marr, Sally Marr, Peter Nicholas Marr, Anna alias Agness Marr infant children of John Marr dec'd do convey the same to George Hairston as they arrive at the age of 21 years unless at that time they shall show good cause why this decree should be set aside.
-Same vs same..said 1200 acres to said George Hairston and also 216 disputed acres.
-King vs Pitman, on a motion of the Defendant to take the deposition of William Dodson, John Dodson; Nehemiah Vernun, Joshua Smith, Robert Means, John King, James Hunter or any three appointed Commissioners for this purpose.
-Penington and Brown vs Hanby and others, Richard Davidson security
-Thomas Hornsby 3 days witness Joseph Newman vs David Going
-Rowan & Scott vs Sutton, Archelaus Hughes Spl Bl
-Joseph Reynolds 1 day witness Harbour vs Corn
-William Frazier same
-Commonwealth vs Fitzgerald dismd
-James Morrison 1 day witness Corn vs Harbour
-Corn vs Harbour dismd

PAGE 213

-Bolt vs Chandler and Wife, William J. Mayo and Samuel Staples Spl Bl
COURT 26 April 1799 present: Francis Turner, Brett Stovall, John Hughes and Peter Scales.
-Saunders vs Ross, Gabriel Penn, George Fulcher Spl Bl
-Sutton vs Webb Not Guilty
-Humphrey Smith 2 days witness Harbour vs Corn
-Benjamin Haile same
-Deed- John Tatum to John Adams
-Penington & Brown vs Hanby and others - dismd
-Keaton vs Haile dismd
-Going vs Keaton, Court of the opinion the Defendant have the benefit of his Judgement.

-Breden	vs	Morgan	contd
-Lyon	vs	Smith	contd
-Ogle	vs	Walter	Judgement
-Smith	vs	Tenison	contd
-Smith	vs	Vest	contd
-Smith	vs	Poteet	"
-Newman	vs	Going	"
-Chitwood	vs	Blankenship	"
-Gilliam	vs	Newman	"
-Going	vs	Going	"
-Trigg	vs	Reynolds	"
-Holand	vs	Lyon	"
-Yoes	vs	Jones	"
-Lewis	vs	Eckolds	:

Page 213 contd

-Keaton vs Lindsay contd
-Lewis vs Jones contd
-Going vs Ellyson dismd
-Laban Going 2 days witness Obadiah Going vs David Going
-Joshua Rentfro, Gabriel Penn and John Hughes appointed to view the Jail and let repairs to the lowest bidder.
-Rowan & Soctt vs Hughes and others, Gabriel Penn Spl Bl
-Breden vs Morgan, referred to Abraham Penn, Jonathan Hanby, Brett Stovall and Peter Scales..their award to be the Judgement of this Court.

PAGE 214

Court doth set and rate the following liquors, diets, etc: rum per gal 16/, wine same, brandy 12/, whiskey 10/, cyder 2/,breakfast 1/3, dinner 1/9, supper 1/3, lodgings 6d, fodder per bdl 2d, sheave oats 3d, corn and oats per gal 9d, stablage 4d, pasturage 6d.

COURT 30 May 1799 present: Edward Tatum, Hamon Critz, Brett Stovall, John Hughes, Peter Scales.

-Deed- William Perkins and wife to Palmer Critchfield
-Deed- Palmer Critchfield to John Branscum
-Deed- William Perkins to Thomas Carr, further proved
-Deed- Bartemus Reynolds to John Adams further proved
-Giles Martin is appointed surveyor of the road from Charles Fosters to the Franklin line in place of Zaphaniah Tenison.
-John Blaze appointed surveyor of the road from the ford of the Mayo River near Henry Francis to Carolina line in place of William Cherry.
-Joseph Reynolds, Alexander Lackey, James Harris, Joseph Willis or any three to view a way for a road around Nathan Hall plantation and report.
-A report of a view of a road from James Harris to James Denny returned.
-Nehemiah Daniel appointed surveyor of the road from Shockleys cabin to the top of the mountain at the Grayson line.
-Hairston vs Devonshire contd
-Peter Hairston vs Michaux contd
-Adams vs Keaton Judgement
-Duvall vs Smith Judgement
-Deed- Joshua Adams to Daniel Adams, Pheby Adams wife of Daniel Adams relinquishes her right of dower.
-Deed- William Witt to William Baker, Elisabeth Witt wife of William Witt relinquishes her right of dower.
-William James Mayo, William Frazier, Jesse Corn, James Morrison or any three appointed to view a way for a road from below John Hancocks to Turners road near the said Mayos.
-Deed of Emancipation from Richard Graves of Dinwiddie County to negro Harry and other slaves therein mentioned, certified under the hand of the Clerk of Court.

PAGE 215

-Deed- John Burnett to Elisha Packwood, further proved
-Deed- Samuel Harris to James Harris
-Robert Hall 1 day witness Adams vs Keaton
-John Mankin same
-James Haile same
-Benjamin Haile same
-Joseph Going same
-Koger vs Sleator Judgement
-On a motion of William Brewer to stay the proceedings of a Judgement obtained against him by William Banks, granted with Sackville Brewer his security.
-Spencer vs Stephens Judgement
-Smith vs Bates abates by return
-Hoof vs Peregoy N.P.

Page 215 contd

-Tucker vs McGaughey dismd
-Deed- Joshua Adams to William Witt, Pheby Adams wife of Joshua Adams relinquishes her right of dower..2 deeds
-Penn vs Miller dismd
-Dalton vs Price Judgement
-Samuel Dalton vs Smith dismd
-Biscoe vs Hale Judgement
-Wilson vs Brewer Judgement
-Banks vs Harris dismd

PAGE 216

COURT 18 June 1799 on the examination of Jonathan Hanby on suspicion of being guilty of the detastable crime of buggery.
Present: Francis Turner, George Penn, Joshua Rentfro, Peter Scales.
Prisoner led to the Bar in custody of Samuel Clark, gentleman Sheriff, and pleads Not Guilty. The Court examined divers witness and the Court is of the opinion that he is Not Guilty and discharged.

COURT 27 June 1799 present: Brett Stovall, Charles Foster, Joseph Stovall, John Hughes.

-Deed- John Hancock and wife to Jacob Mayo. Elisabeth Hancock wife of John Hancock relinquishes her right of dower and the same is ordered to be certified and sent to the Clerk of Fluvanna Court and charged to Jesse Corn.
-Deed- John Hanby to John Hughes
A report of a view of a road from a little below John Hancocks into the road leading from the Turners to the Courthouse it is ordered David Harbour and his gang clear and open.
-Nathan Morrison appointed surveyor of the road from Francis Turners to the top of Bull Mountain in place of William James Mayo.
-Booth vs Staples & Co for the benefit of Joseph Breden referred to Charles Foster, William James Mayo and Jesse Corn.
-Deed- Jonathan Hanby to William Mitchell
-Banks vs Mapes Judgement
-Deed- John Hughes to Jonathan Hanby and David Hanby, 2 deeds
-Booth vs Staples & Co. for B. Breden
-Deed- William Carter to William Mitchell
-Deed- William Mitchell to William Buckley, Treasurer of Virginia.

PAGE 217

COURT 25 July 1799 present: William Banks, Charles Thomas, George Penn, Joseph Stovall.

-Deed- William Dabney and wife to Daniel Askew further proved
-Joshua Rentfro and Charles Thomas appointed to view the repairs to the Jail.
-James Taylor foreman, John Miller, Jesse Corn, John Ferrell, Daniel Adams, John Medley Jr, David Taylor, James Thompson, Peter Frans, Richard Davidson, William Fitzgerald, William Sharp, Moses Reynolds, James Hale, Clifton Keaton and Joseph Going to serve as Grand Jury.
-Deed- Benjamin Morris to John Wilson certified from the Clerk of Montgomery County.
-Hanby vs Bennett
-Hanby vs Fagin
Present: Hamon Critz, Charles Foster, John Hughes, Jonathan Hanby, Joshua Rentfro, Edward Tatum, William Carter, Stephen Lyon and Francis Turner are recommended as fit persons to serve as Sheriff.
-Deed- Abner Eckolds to Jasiel Eckolds, Talmon Harbour to pay.
-Gabriel Penn presented 3 lists of insolvents for the year 1798, one for land, one for property and the other for tithes.
-Penington vs Hanby and others
-Brown vs Hanby and others
-Sheriff to pay Gabriel Penn 5.19.6
-Laban Going is allowed 1 day witness Oba. Going vs David Going

Page 217 contd

-John Dalton, Commissioner of the County, $70. for services
-Tatum & Co vs Yoes, Samuel Clark Jr Spl Bl
-Hanby vs Davidson dismd

PAGE 218

George Penn, Joshua Rentfro, William Banks, Edward Tatum or any three are appointed to let to the lowest bidder the rebuilding of the Jail.

COURT 26 July 1799 present: Francis Turner, Edward Tatum, Charles Thomas, Joshua Rentfro.

-Smith vs Tenison, Court orders and decrees that the Defendant pay the Complainant $20. with interest @ 5% per annum from 26 July 1796 till paid.
-Lyon vs Smith, jury sworn: David Taylor, James Turner, George Fulcher, William Fitzgerald, John Miller, Daniel Fain, James Haile, Samuel Corn, William Hannah, Edward Lewis, Daniel Sleator, William Deal Sr.. a juror withdrew and continued.
-Holand vs Lyon dismd
-Samuel Clark Jr 2 days witness Lyon vs Holand
-Gabriel Penn same
-Newman vs Going, referred to Nathaniel Smith and John Parr
-King vs Pitman, 3 suits, dismd
-White vs Tatum contd
-James Lyon Jr 2 days witness Newman vs Gilliam
-Jesse Tatum Sr same
-Smith vs Vest Judgement
-Hale vs Lemmon, referred to Joshua Rentfro and Daniel Fain
-Laban Going 1 day witness Oba. Going vs D. Going
-William Hannah 2 days witness Hale vs Lemmon
-John Chapman same
-William Fitzgerald same
-Jacob Critz same
-Joseph Keaton same
-John Miller same
-John Fletcher same
-Munford Smith same
-Judith Keaton same
-Judith Going same

PAGE 219

COURT 29 August 1799 present: Edward Tatum, John Hughes, Joshua Rentfro, William Banks.

-Deed- John Dillion to William Bellamay
-Deed- William Perkins to Palmer Critchfield, further proved
-Deed- Nathaniel Stewart to David May
-Deed- Leander Dehart, Thomas Tenison, Mary Tenison, James Dehart, Catharine Dehart, Susanah Dehart and Mary Dehart to Mathew Stanton produced and ordered to be sent to the Clerk of Amherst County.
-Deed- Samuel Harris to James Harris further proved
-Report of a view of a road from Francis Turners to the Meeting House was returned.
-James Turner qualified as Captain of the Militia
-Thomas R. Hall qualified as Lt. of Militia
-William Carter, Munford Smith, Robert Green, William Green or any three to view a road from the top of the mountain at Bells Spur to the North Carolina line.
-Staples assignee vs Miller dismd
-Perkins vs Brewer, take deposition of Samuel Strong, William Peay, William Dearing, Thomas Rivers, James Daniel and Zachariah Snead or any three appointed Commissioners for said purpose.
-James Harris appointed surveyor of the road from his house into the Courthouse Road near Francis Turners.
-Deed- Gabriel Penn to John Hughes

Page 219 contd

-Jones vs Lewis on a Delivery Bond, Judgement
-Brewer vs Banks, Court of the opinion Complainant be entitled to the benefit of a credit which is already credited to John Staples.
-Hairston vs Devonshire contd
-Hairston vs Michaux contd
-On a motion of James Nowlin against Levi Peregoy stating that he neglects and misuses by not furnishing the proper necessaries of life for a certain child named _____ and it appearing to the satisfaction of the Court that the child is misused; hterefore, it is ordered that the said Levy Peregoy be summoned to this Court to show excuse why the child is so misused and not furnished with the proper necessaries of life.

PAGE 220

-Michaux vs Hughes contd
-Staples vs Critz Judgement
-Tatum vs Going contd
-Nowlin for the benefit of___ vs Nowlin contd
-Hoff vs Perigoy N.P.
-Moore vs Going contd
-John Miller 1 day witness at a different Court
-Jacob Michaux vs Abijah Hughes
-Hughes vs Sowder N.P.
-George Clark recommended as a fit and proper person to serve as 2nd Lt. under Gabriel Penn, Capt of Artillery in the place of John Dalton who hath resigned.
-John Hughes appointed to take care of the Courthouse in place of Gabriel Penn, who resigned.

PAGE 221

COURT 6 September 1799 on the examination of William Turman on suspicion of feloniously stealing and carting off an anvil, the property of D. Morgan.
Present: George Penn, Joshua Rentfro, Hamon Critz, John Hughes and Edward Tatum.
Prisoner was led to the Bar in the custody of Samuel Clark, gentleman sheriff, and plead not guilty..found Not Guilty.

COURT 26 September 1799 present: Abraham Penn, Samuel Packwood, Gabriel Penn, George Penn, Charles Foster, Charles Thomas, John Hughes, Joshua Rentfro, William Banks, Joseph Stovall, Brett Stovall.

-Deed- Stephen Chalton from Joseph Pratt
-Jacob Lindsay qualified as Deputy Sheriff under Samuel Clark.
-Gabriel Penn qualified as Justice of the Peace for the County
-Deed- Samuel Clark Sr to Gabriel Penn
-Deed- James Pemberton to Jacob Hickman
-Deed- John Hughes to John Hanby
-Overseers of the Poor bind out Stephen Cisney 7 years of age to Stephen Cesney his grandfather.
-Hairston vs Devonshire contd
-P. Hairston vs Michaux Judgement
-Deed- Jonathan Ison to James Harris
-Going vs Going, referred to James Gains, Stephen Lyon
-Penington vs Hanby and others
-Brown vs Hanby and other dismd
-A view of a road from the top of Bull Mountain iinto the road below Blackberry Creek returned. Ordered Ignatious Looksey and his gang call on Ignatious Sims and John Gossett and their hands to open same.
-John Stone is appointed surveyor of the road from Critz new buildings to the Henry line in place of Sackville Brewer Jr.

PAGE 222

-William Hensley is appointed surveyor of the road from Obadiah Hudsons to the Grayson line in place of William Williams.
-Ordered that the hands of George Hairston at the Mayo Store and at Griffins, Henry Kogers hands, Abraham Penns hands at his quarter and Samuel Coleman Morris and his be added to Bowls Abingtons list and hereby discharged from all other roads.
-Report of a view of a road from around Nathan Halls plantation be recorded.
-Michaux vs Hughes Judgement
-Isaac Adams 5 days witness Michaux vs Hughes
-John Miller 1 day for same
-Ordered that Adam Turner and his gang to clear and open the road from Francis Turners to the Meeting House.
-On a petition of Brett Stovall, Gentleman Surveyor, William Adams is admitted as his Deputy and H. Smith to examine him as to his abilities.
-Tatum vs Going contd
-William Adams qualified as Deputy Surveyor
-Smith vs Corn September Court
-Power of Attorney of John Fletcher Sr to John Fletcher Jr recorded.
-Greensville Penn appointed Commissioner of the County.
-William James Mayo, James Turner, Alexander Lackey are appointed to procession all the lands in Capt. James Turners Company.

PAGE 223

COURT 31 August 1799 present; Charles Thomas, George Penn, Joshua Rentfro, Joseph Stovall, Hamon Critz, William Carter.

-On examination of Ralph Danger on suspicion of stealing a bell. The prisoner was led to the Bar in custody of Samuel Clark, Gentleman Sheriff, plead not guilty. Court find him Not Guilty.

COURT Thursday 31 October 1799 present: Joshua Rentfro, Francis Turner, William Carter, Charles Thomas, George Penn.

-Deed- Thomas Bristoe to Featherston Walden, further proved
-Cradock vs Tenison dismd
-Deed- John Breden Sr to Jeremiah Burnett Jr, Jane Breden wife of John Breden relinquishes her right of dower.
-Skillern assignee vs Long, Hugh Poor Spl Bl
-Price vs Walden dismd
-John Wilson appointed Constable in place of Laughlin Fagin who resigned.
-George Aylsworth recommended as Lt in place of Mitchell Thompson
-William Carlin recommended as Ensgin in place of Woodson Hamons
-Deed- Thomas P. Jorden to Peter Saunders, further proved
-Deed- Rowland Salman to William Sneed
-Augustine Thomas foreman, John Fletcher, Moses Reynolds, Joseph Going, Peter Frans, Jesse Corn, John Miller, David Rogers, Beveridge Hughes, David Morgan, Barnard M. Price, Edward Lewis, James Thomson, John Spencer, Moses Hurt, William Fitzgerald to serve as Grand Jury.
-Turner vs Spauldin dismd
-George Penn and Greensville Penn vs Marlow, Samuel Clark Spl Bl
-Charles Thomas, John Hall and William Fuson are appointed to procession all the lands within the bounds of Capt. George Lackeys Company of Militia.
-John Allen and Thomas Allen vs Archelaus Hughes

PAGE 224

-Jacob Critz, Joseph Commings and Augustine Thomas are appointed to procession all the lands within the bounds of Critz Company of Militia.
-On a motion of John Hanby and David Hanby leave is granted them to keep an Ordinary in their Tavern in Taylorsville, Samuel Staples their security.
-James Dickerson, William Cloud and James Carlin are appointed to procession all the land in Tho mas Whitlocks Company of Militia.

Page 224 contd

-William Carter, William Green and James L. Gains are appointed to procession all the land in Capt. William Moores Company of Militia.
-NathanielSmith, John Tatum and Joshua Rentfro to procession all the land in Samuel Staples Company of Militia.
-Reynolds vs Lee dismd
-Hughes vs Brewer Jr, John Miller Spl Bl
-William Carter appeared in Court and produced a Commission appointing him Sheriff with George Carter, William Banks, John Hughes, George Penn, Brett Stovall, Jonathan Hanby, Joshua Rentfro, Archelaus Hughes and Hamon Critz as his securities.

COURT Friday 1 November 1799 present: Francis Turner, Edward Tatum, Hamon Critz, Brett Stovall.

-John Allen and Thomas Allen vs A. Hughes, Bond defective
-Going vs Burge dismd
-Danger vs Martindill dismd
-Hughes vs Fagin, John Bennett Spl Bl
-Commonwealth vs Fagin not guilty
-Nowlin vs Price dismd
-Wilson vs Danger, Daniel Martindill Spl Bl, Nathaniel Smith further Spl Bl
-Going vs Going, referees discharged, redocket
-White vs Tatum Contd
-An account of draughts and expenditures in the Militia returned by Col. Penn.

PAGE 225

County of Patrick for the year 1799

Clerks annual salary	25.
Sheriffs annual salary	25.
Deputy States Attorney salary	25.
Eliphaz Shelton for hauling timber	1.25
Jesse Corn for 2 young wolf heads	4.16
Charles Foster 1 old wolf head	4.16
same for Thomas Mitchell	4.16
same for same	4.16
John Foster 1 old wolf head	4.16
S. Staples assignee for James Nowlin, same	4.16
same	4.16
same for Moses Hurt	4.16
	109.53

-Ward & Calaway vs Tenison dismd
-Lawson vs Rogers, Harvey Fitzgerald Spl Bl
-Lyon vs Smith, jury sworn: Harvey Fitzgerald, James Nowlin, Pleasant C. Reynolds, John Lavender, Jesse Corn, James Dearman, William French, John Allen, Humphrey Smith, Richard Gains, William Rogers, Alexander Burge... Verdict for Defendant, new tryal granted.
-Deed- Thomas Willis to George Corn
-A certificate from under the hand of George Penn, J.P., certifying that Greensville Penn took the oath of a Commissioner.
-On a motion of Brett Stovall, one of the Overseers of the Poor, on behalf of Jane Barton vs Isaac Dodson and David Rogers his security, for the support of a bastard child of said Jane Barton. Rogers appeared in Court and confessed Judgement for 5 pounds and it being the first years maintenance of said child, together with costs of this motion, lawyer fees excepted.
-Edward Tatum 2 days witness Fagin vs Commonwealth
-Edward Tatum 2 days witness Lyon vs Smith
-Wilson vs Danger not guilty
-William Lyon 1 day witness Tatum vs White
-David Rogers 1 day witness Gilliam vs Newman
-Lyon vs Smith, on a motion of the Plaintiff leave is granted him to amend his declaration on paying such extraordinary costs to Defendant as may occur thereby same is remanded to the Rules for further

Page 225 contd

proceedings.
-John Bridgman 2 days witness Wilson vs Danger
-John Martindill same
-Daniel Martindill same
-Charles Sneed same
-Joshua Rentfro 1 day witness Keaton vs Hale

PAGE 226

-Hale vs Simmons ward Judgement

COURT 26 November 1799 present: William Banks, Hamon Critz, Edward Tatum, Gabriel Penn, John Hughes.

-Deed- Richard Thomas to John James
-Power of attorney of Mary Price and William Price to Larkin Price
-Deed of Trust- Joseph Reynolds to Obadiah Burnett
-Ordered the Sheriff pay William Hannah 88¢ for overcharge.
-Hairston vs Devonshire contd
-Tatum assignee vs Going contd
-Nowlin vs Nowlin contd
-Perkins vs Brewer Jr Judgement
-Randolph Adams allowed 1 day 25 miles witness Perkins vs Brewer
-William Banks 2 days for same
-William Fuson qualified as Ensign of Militia
-Ordered that James Harris call on William Sneed andDavid Roberson and their gangs to open and clear the road viewed from the said James Harris into the road leading from Francis Turners to Maburys Gap.
-William Carter produced a Commission and qualified as Sheriff.
-Benjamin Philpott is appointed to take care of the Courthouse and do necessary repairs and appointed Jailor by the Sheriff.
-William Banks, Elijah Banks, Thomas Banks qualified as Deputy Sheriffs.
-Smith vs McNanney contd
-Perkins vs Dehart Judgement
-Gilmore exors vs Bolling contd
-Jacob Lindsay and Samuel Clark Jr Qualified to collect the arrears of Samuel Clark, late sheriff.

PAGE 227

COURT 30 January 1800 present: Edward Tatum, Charles Foster, John Hughes, Gabriel Penn.

-Deed- Thomas Barten to Samuel Hunt??
-Deed- Charles Crutcher to Peter Frans
-Deed- Elias Bryant to William Parsons
-Banks vs Gilbert Judgement
-Deed- David Morgan to William Roberson
-Deed- Nathaniel Stewart to William Perkins, further proved
-Deed of Trust- Tederick Yoes to Gabriel Penn and Samuel Clark Jr
-Deed- Charles Foster attorney in fact for Timothy Stamps to John Kendrick Sr
-Harris vs Lewis and Penn
-Hughes vs Harris dismd
-Joseph Garrett is appointed surveyor of the road from the Grayson line to the North Carolina line down the Bell Spur.
-Ordered that Joseph Garrett call on Peter Bellow and his hands, Bartlett Smith and his, William Henslie and his and they do clear the road viewd from the Grayson line, Bell Spur to the Carolina line.
-Carlin and others vs Braneum dismd
-Robert Hudspeth appointed Overseer of the Poor in place of John Nunns.
-James Miller is exempt from the payment of County and Parish levies for the future.

Page 227 contd

County Levy for the year 1799 brought fwd	109.53
S. Staples for Daniel Fain, 1 old wolf head	4.16
Clerk for service to Commissioners	40.
S. Staples for Benjamin Philpott for repairs to the Courthouse	13.21
Depositium for use of County	50.
Sheriff for collecting same	13.16
	230.06

-Deed of Trust, Joseph Reynolds to Obadiah Burner..(Burnett??) and Francis Turner trustees, further proved
-Henry Fry appeared in Court with Ribert Green his security to be of good behavior for 12 months 1 day towards Elihu Ayrs.

PAGE 228

-Edward Lewis an invalid pensioner, wounds received in the late War, Court of the opinion that his pension should continue inthe amount of $50.00.
-Ordered the Overseers of the Poor bind out Elijah Salsberry, 13 years of age, an orphan to David Roberson.
-Overseers of the Poor to bind out Francis Allenson 13 years of age.
-Smith vs McNanney, John Akers owes the Defendant 150 pounds in trade. Provide he gets a fee simple title to a certain tract sold him by the Defendant and costs.

COURT 27 February 1800 present: Joshua Rentfro, Charles Foster, John Hughes, Charles Thomas, Edward Tatum, Brett Stovall.

-Deed- Martin Amos to Moses Harbour
-Deed- David Morgan and wife to William Roberson, further proved
-Deed- James Armstrong to Jacob McCraw
-Deed- David May to William Burress
-Deed- John Stewart and wife to Abraham Hawks
-Deed- Martin Talley and wife and Joseph Johnson and wife to Isaac Branscum.
-Deed- John Hubbard to Stephen Mayner
-Power of attorney ________, Jane Hubbard to John Hubbard.
-John Turner qualified as Lt. of Militia
-Deed- Lee Hughes to John Hughes
-On a motion of James Turner to build a water grist mill across Rock Castle Creek, he owns land on both sides.
-Hairston vs Chitwood Judgement
-Hughes vs Davidson Judgement
-Penn vs Smith
-Penn vs Parr

PAGE 229

-Deed- Archelaus Hughes and Jonathan Hanby to John Hughes
-Deed- Buckannun Dunlop and Co to John Hughes
-Hairston vs Pigg Judgement
-Deed- Nathan Hall to William Call
-Breden vs Morgan, deposition of Peter Sealy and John Breden Sr to be taken.
-Hughes vs Harvey Fitzgerald Judgement
-Penn vs Harvey Fitzgerald Judgement
-Laban Going 5 days wintess Obadiah Going vs David Going
-Susanah Danger 3 days witness Danger vs Wilson
-Nancy Danger same
-Skillern assigne vs Long Judgement
-Newman vs Going, award returned for Defendant
-Yoes vs Jones dismd
-Critz vs Bush and others, ordered that the said land in the Bill be vested in Complainant and that the Defendants, Coonrod Bush, Charles Walker, Willis Walker and Mason Walker do execute deeds the better to assure his title.

Page 229 contd

-Augustine Thomas foreman, Jesse Corn, John Spencer, James Inniss, John Adams, George Penn Sr, James L. Gains, Isham Cradock, Richard Pilson, Peter Frans, Abram Hawks, Joseph Johnson, David Taylor, Humphrey Smith, William Sublett are to serve as Grand Jury.
-A recc----- from Obadiah Burnett to Joseph Reynolds.

PAGE 230

COURT 28 February 1800 present: Edward Tatum, Hamon Critz, Charles Thomas, Charles Foster, Brett Stovall

-Penn vs Michaux and others Judgement
-Perkins vs Brewer Jr Judgement
-P. Hairston vs Michaux
-Ellyson vs Marrs representatives ordered that the Surveyor of the County attend Court 1st Monday in April relating to the last of the Complainant.
-White vs Tatum contd
-Gilliam vs Newman contd
-David Hanby 2 days witness White vs Tatum
-John Parr 1 day witness Gilliam vs Newman
-Lewis vs Eckolds
-Chitwood vs Blankenship
-Holand vs Lyon dismd
-Lewis vs Critz Judgement
-Trigg vs Reynolds same
-Rowan & Scott vs Sutton, jury sworn: Christopher Long, John Hall, Harvey Fitzgerald, Henry Frans, Humphrey Smith, Jesse Corn, John Wilson, Thomas Mitchell, Richard Davidson, Jacob Critz, Peter Frans, Samuel Morris, verdict for Pltf for debt, one penny damages.
-Bolt vs Chandler & Company, same jury, verdict for Pltf.
-Sutton vs Webb dismd
-Going vs Newman same
-Deed- William Carter and Samuel Staples attorneys in fact for Woolman Studham to Elijah Dehart.
-Administration of the estate of Federick Fitzgerald granted to George Penn and Harvey Fitzgerald, Samuel Staples as security.
-Samuel Clark Sr, Samuel Clark Jr, Gabriel Penn, Peter Frans to appraise said estate.
-Mrs. Thomas relinquishes her right of dower in a deed to J. James conveyed by her husband.
-Barnard M. Price vs James Morrison dismd

PAGE 231

-John Gates 2 days witness Hanby vs Tatum
-Susanah Gates same
-Lewis vs Eckolds, ordered that the Defendant Abner Eckolds or his son Jasiel Eckolds do convey to the Complainant or to Jacob Adams Sr title to the said lands.
-John Adams 2 days witness Daniel Adams vs Nowlin
-Giles Martin same
-Joseph Ross 3 days witness Keaton vs Haile
-Patsey Ross same
-Joseph Keaton 1 day for same
-Judith Keaton same
-Ralph Danger 2 days witness for Hanby vs Tatum
-Susanah Danger 1 day witness Danger vs Wilson
-Nancy Danger same
-Keaton vs Lindsay
-Edward Tatum 2 days witness Fagin vs Commonwealth

COURT 27 March 1800 present: Charles Thomas, Edward Tatum, Joseph Stovall, Gabriel Penn

-Deed- John Hubbard to Stephen Maynor further proved
-Deed- Joseph Miller to John Akers

Page 231 contd

-Deed- Edward Lewis to William Walden
-Deed- Blizard Magruder to George Clark
-Deed- Samuel Clark Sr to George Clark
-Deed- Blizard Magruder to Gabriel Penn
-Smith vs Branham Judgement
-Deed- William Barton to James Epperson
-Deed- George Hairston and Joshua Rentfro to William Jones
-Deed- William Jones to Charles Crutcher
-Deed- Joseph Reynolds to Isaac Collings
-Deed- Joseph Reynolds to Stephen Harper
-Going vs Going
-Smith vs Maynor

PAGE 232

-On a motion of Jacob Michaux an injunction to stay the proceedings obtained against him by Peter Hairston was over ruled
-Adams vs Bolling dismd
-Gilmer vs Bolling Judgement
-Randals vs Pyrtle dismd
-Hairston vs Devonshire contd
-Deed- William Armstrong to William Smith
-Deed- Thomas Gee and wife to Joseph Reynolds
-Smith vs Blackborne, Judgement
-Smith vs Frazier
-Tatum vs Going
-Smith vs McNanney
-Nolin vs Nowlen
-Hoof vs Perigoy
-Anglin vs Brewer Jr Judgement
-Hannah vs Mannin
-Rainey vs Going Judgement
-French vs Brewer Jr same
-Deed- Leander Hughes to John Hughes, further proved
-French vs Hughes Judgement
-William Adams 1 day witness Going vs Tatum
-Deed- Richardson Herndon to John Spencer
-Lee vs Blackburn referred to John Breden Jr, Alexander Lackey.
-James Harris 1 day witness Lee vs Blackbourne
-Martha Harris same
-Abel Perigoy 1 day witness Walden vs Whalin
-Jacob Blackbourne 1 day for same
-Tatum vs Going referred to George Penn, Joshua Rentfro, Brett Stovall and John Hughes
-Lewis vs Going Judgement
-Nowlan vs Nowlan, ordered Richard Nowland be summoned to appear next Court and show cause (if any he can) why he should not be fined for his non appearance.
-Going vs Cummings dismd
-Price vs Jones Judgement
-Reynolds vs Michaux same
-James Nowland 4 days witness Nowlan vs Nowlan
-George Hairston vs Frans contd
-Penn vs Garrott dismd
-Penn vs Carlin Judgement
-Penn vs Jones dismd
-Penn vs Hanby dismd

PAGE 233

-Deed- David Rogers to Pleasant C. Reynolds
-Samuel Hooker appointed surveyor of the road from Patrick Courthouse into the road below William Carters at Little Dan.
-Cooke vs Mapes Judgement
-Ayrs vs Mapes same
-Banks vs Quarles contd
-Robert Sharp 2 days witness John Nowlin vs Francis Nowlin

Page 233 contd

-Charles Thomas 2 days witness John Nowlin vs Francis Nowlin
-Koger vs Bolling contd
-P. Hairston vs Michaux
-Creasey vs Biggs
-John Fletcher, James Epperson, Joseph Going and George Fulcher or any three appointed to view a way for a road from Bartons old place into the road at the old sign post.
-Stovall vs Stephens dismd
-Griffin vs Koger
-Hairston vs P. Rickman Jr
-John Hughes vs Job Lowder and William Harris
-Hairston vs Abington
-Mitchell vs Tatum
-Whalen vs Waldon

COURT 15 April 1800 present: Hamon Critz, Joseph Stovall, Gabriel Penn, John Hughes, Jonathan Hanby.

-On the examination of a negro woman slave named Lidda on suspicion of burning the dwelling house of Peter Findley. Prisoner led to the Bar in the custody of William Carter, Gentleman Sheriff, plead not guilty...Court of the opinion the prisoner is Guilty and to receive 25 lashes on her bare back and then set at liberty.
-Jones vs Yoes

PAGE 234

COURT 24 April 1800 present: Francis Turner, Edward Tatum, Charles Thomas, Charles Foster

-Nathan Hall, Gentleman, appeared in Court and produced credentials of his being in Communion with the Baptist Society, Edward Tatum his security.
-James Taylor foreman, Joel Harbour, Thomas Hollandsworth, Moses Godard, Samuel Clark Jr, Alexander Lackey, Nathaniel Ross, Richard Mills, Moses Walden, Charles Rakes, Thomas Dillard, John Finney, John Fletcher, John Crum, Joel Chitwood, Edward Lewis to serve as Grand Jury.
-Deed- Richard Massey to Edward Lewis
-Deed- Edward Lewis to John Mize
-Deed- John Rea to James Taylor
-Penn vs William Fitzgerald Judgement
-Going vs Rea dismd
-Going and wife vs Rea same
-Griffin vs Bundurant same
-Deed- John Lee to Edmund Brammer further proved
-Deed of Trust- Joel Chitwood to George Penn further proved
-Deed- Blizard Magruder to George Penn
-White vs Tatum, jury sworn: James Fulkerson, John Turner, Peter Frans, William Harris, James Haile, Samuel Hunt, William Fuson, John Adams, Burgess Brammer, William Stone, Elias Bryant, Daniel Adams..verdict returned for Pltf.
-Samuel Hunt is exempt from the payment of County and Parish levies for the future.
-Deed- Benjamin Yeates to Jarrott Bransom
-Lee vs Blackborne
-Lewis vs Jones
-Saunders vs Ross
-Frans vs Banks
Tatum vs Penington
-Chitwood vs Blankenship
-William Lyon 1 day and 6 miles witness Tatum vs White
- same 1 day 6 miles witness Newman vs Gilliam
-Rowan & Scott vs Hughes and others, jury sworn: James Fulkerson, John Turner, James Haile, Samuel Hunt, Nathaniel Ross, Alexander Lackey, Edward Lewis, Burgess Brammer, William Harris, William Keaton, William Fuson, John Adams..Verdict for Pltf..appeal granted Defendant.

PAGE 235

-White vs Tatum
-James Taylor allowed 5 days witness Wilson vs Danger
-Roland Salman 1 day 22 miles witness Adams vs Nowlin
-James Hall 1 day same
-Richard Massey same
-Giles Martin same
-John Adams same
-John Ingram same
-Levi Pedigo same
-Burgess Brammer same
-Absalom Hancock same
-Charles Rakes same
-Elisabeth Spaulden 1 day witness William Harris vs E. Bryant
-Cunningham & Co vs Rakes, William Banks Spl Bl
-James McCutchen 1 day witness Daniel Adams vs James Nowlin
-Edward Lewis 3 days witness Breden vs Morgan
-John Wilson Jr vs Danger, jury sworn: Sackville Brewer Jr, William Fuson, Nathaniel Ross, Christopher Long, William Keaton, Jesse Corn, Edward Lewis, Robert Sharp, Burgess Brammer, Charles Rakes, John Adams, John Mankins....verdict returned for Pltf.
-William Fitzgerald 1 day witness Haile vs Keaton
-Mary Fitzgerald same
-Richard Davidson 5 days witness Tatum vs Smith
-John Bridgman 2 days witness Wilson vs Danger
-John Collings same
-Charles Sneed same
-George Penn 2 days witness Wilson vs Tatum
-Sackville Brewer Jr 5 days for same
-Saunders & Co vs Dehart, William Fuson Special Bail

PAGE 236

COURT 25 April 1800 present: Abraham Penn, Charles Foster, Charles Thomas, George Penn

-Tatum vs Penington, jury sworn: Larkin Price, Joseph Keaton, Daniel Adams, William Fitzgerald, Nathaniel Ross, William Keaton, George Fulcher, Burgess Brammer, Charles Rakes, James Nowlin, Joseph Newman, John Adams...Verdict returned for Pltf.
-Chitwood vs Blankenship, jury same as above, verdict for Pltf.
-Eliphaz Shelton 4 days witness Chitwood vs Blankenship
-Keay?? assignee vs Walden, jury sworn: Sackville Brewer, John Fulkerson, Archelaus Hughes, David Hanby, Jesse Corn, William Adams, Richard Gains, John Hanby, Eliphaz Shelton, Roland Salmon, James McCutchen, James Haile...verdict for Pltf.
-Tatum vs Smith Not Guilty
-Tatum & Co vs Yoes, jury sworn: Larkin Price, Joseph Keaton, Daniel Adams, William Fitzgerald, William Keaton, Nathaniel Ross, Burgess Brammer, Charles Rakes, James Nowlin, John Adams, James Deal.. Verdict for Pltf.
-French vs Brewer - Judgement for L25.5.1½ with interest, also a suit in Henry County listed as Brewer vs Bassett.
-Wilson Sr vs Danger, deposition of Caty Coomer, William Coomer, Joseph Cloud be taken, Mathew Moore, Jack Martin, James Lyon Sr, James Lyon Jr and Thomas Guins or any three appointed as Commissioners to take said depositions. John Wilson Jr as security.
-Blaze by his next friend vs Amos
-Hughes vs Fagin
-Posey for benefit of B. Penn vs Hughes Administrators
-Hughes vs Brewer
-Banks vs Frans, jury sworn: Sackville Brewer, John Tatum, John Hanby, Richard Gains, James McCutchen, William Adams, Jesse Corn, David Hanby, Roland Salman, James Deal, John Fulkerson..verdict returned for the Pltf.
-Mrs Ely Lyon wife of Stephen Lyon, came into Court and relinquished her right of dower to a tract of land conveyed by her husband to Joshua Rentfro.

PAGE 237

-Moses Walden 2 days witness William Harris vs E. Bryant
-Elisabeth Spauldin 1 day for same
-Roland Lee 2 days same
-Richard Massey 1 day for same
-Nathan Hall same
-James Hall 1 day witness Adams vs Nowlin
-Roland Salman same
-Levy Pedigo same
-John Adams same
-Absalom Hancock same
-Charles Rakes same
-Burgess Brammer same
-Giles Martin same
-John Ingram same
-James McCutchen same
-Breden vs Morgan, take deposition of Francis Turner and Peter Saunders Sr.
-Charles Thomas 2 days witness Adams vs Nowlin
-Nowlin vs Adams, on a motion of the Defendant that the Defendant be admitted to file a Bill of Exception to the opinion of this Court.
-Joel Harbour 2 days witness Nowlin vs Adams
-Jesse Corn same
-Nowlin vs L. Price dismd
-Nowlin vs B. M. Price dismd
-Chitwood vs Blankenship
-James Nowlin 2 days witness Harris vs Bryan(t)
-John Bridgman 1 day witness Wilson vs Danger
-George Corn 1 day witness Haile vs Keaton
-Dolley Corn same
-Joseph Ross same
-Patsey Ross same
-Susanah Gates 2 days witness Hanby vs Tatum
-William Carter, Gentleman Sheriff, came into Court and objected to the sufficiency of the jail.
-Ellyson vs Marrs heirs
-Hanby vs Marrs heirs
-Penington vs Hanby and others
-John Wilson 3 days witness Fagin vs Hanby
-John Gates 2 days witness Hanby vs Tatum
-John Burnett same
-Malichia Cummings 1 day witness Keaton vs Haile
-John Bennett 2 days witness Fagin vs Hanby
-William Fitzgerald 2 days witness Haile vs Keaton
-Mary Fitzgerald, his wife, same

PAGE 238

COURT 26 April 1800 present: Abraham Penn, Gabriel Penn, John Hughes, Joseph Stovall, Edward Tatum

-Keaton vs Haile
-Keaton vs J. Haile and wife
-Hanby vs Fagin
-Hanby vs Bennett
-Tatum vs Smith
-Smith vs Poteet and others
-Going vs Newman
-Commonwealth vs L. Fagin
-Calaway & Ward vs Roberson
-Hanby vs Tatum
-Hanby vs Tatum and wife
-Harris vs Marrs heirs
-Skillern assignee vs Long
-Lyon vs Smith
-Harris vs Bryant, jury sworn: Thomas Mitchell, George Carter, Humphrey Smith, William Smith, John Mankin, John Hanby, Eliphaz Shelton, Andrew Joyce, David Hanby, Samuel Hunt, James Epperson, Nathaniel Smith. Verdict for Pltf.

PAGE 238 contd

-Richard Massey 1 day witness William Harris vs Bryant
-Elisabeth Spaulden same
-Nathan Hall same
-Roland Lee same
-James Nowlin same
-Giles Martin same
-Moses Walden same
-Lyon vs Smith
-Harris vs Marrs representatives

PAGE 239

COURT 29 May 1800 present: Charles Thomas, Edward Tatum, Hamon Critz, John Hughes.

-Mitchell vs Rickman
-Reynolds vs Michaux and Brewer Jr
-Deed- Charles Perkins to Samuel Corn
-Deed- John Hanby and David Hanby to Thomas Mitchell - 2 deeds
-Harris Carter 1 day witness Koger vs Bolling
-Robert Lockhart same
-Charles Thomas made a report on processioning and was allowed 14 days.
-John Hall same for 17½ days
-Deed- Charles Thomas to Charles Thomas Jr
-Deed- Detherick Yoes to Meredy Smith
-Banks vs Hensley
-Banks vs Pratt
-John Burnett, John Hall, George Lackey, Silas Ratliff or any three to view a way for a road from the ford of Smith River by Joseph Reynolds into the road next to the Widow Foleys.
-A view of a road from the corner of Eppersons fence into the road at the same post returned and ordered that the same persons before mentioned except John Fletcher and in his place Daniel Fain and they do review the same.
-Hoff vs Pedigo referred to Charles Thomas and John Hall.
-A view of a road from Benjamin Mize to the ford of Smith River at Daniel Ross is admitted and ordered that James Ingram Sr, Abel Pedigo, James Cox, David Ross or any three of them are to view same.
-On a motion of Sackville Brewer Jr and Brett Stovall an injunction to stay the proceedings obtained against them by John Early. granted.
-Sarah Hord 1 day and 24 miles witness Hoff vs Pedigo
-George Penn, Hamon Critz, Jacob Critz, Francis Turner and Joseph Stovall appointed Commissioners to take deposition and examine the Polls of the contest between John Frans and John Hughes.
-Rowan & Scott vs Danger, Defendant came not, Judgement for Pltf.
-David Branham appeared in Court, Complainant John Breden Sr not appearing, discharged.
-Gabriel Penn, Peter Scales, James Taylor, Joseph Stovall and Hamon Critz are appointed Commissioners to examine the Polls of the contest between Joshua Rentfro and John Hughes.
-Sheriff to pay Edward Philpott $1.12 for an overcharge.

PAGE 240

COURT 29 May 1800 present: Charles Thomas, Joseph Stovall, Hamon Critz and John Hughes.

-On the examination of Josiah Bryant on suspicion of taking two cows then in the possession of William Banks, Deputy Sheriff. Prisoner was led to the Bar..Court of the opinion that he be bound to his good behavior 12 months 1 day with Joseph Reynolds, John Sharp Jr as his security.
Present same Court Jonathan Hanby in place of Charles Thomas.
-On the examination of William King on suspicion of stealing a parcel of money from Perkins. Found Not Guilty.

Page 240 contd

COURT 30 May 1800
-On the examination of Laughlin Fagin on suspicion of stealing an axe the property of Joseph Going. Prisoner plead Not Guilty. The Court is of the opinion he is Not Guilty.
Present for the above: Stephen Lyon, Hamon Critz, Joseph Stovall and John Hughes.

PAGE 241

COURT Friday 30 May 1800 present: Edward Tatum, Hamon Critz, Joseph Stovall.

-Deed- William Hopkins to John Hughes
-James Miller 1 day witness Fagin vs Commonwealth
-Jacob Blackborne 2 days witness William Walden vs Thomas Whalen
-Abel Pedigo same
-Hairston vs Devonshire contd
-Nowlin for the benefit of Saunders vs Nowlin
-Hannah vs Manning
-Richard Nowlin 2 days witness John Nowlin vs Francis Nowlin
-Hairston vs Frans
-Deed- Archelaus Hughes to Haley Talley
-Banks vs Quarles
-Koger vs Bolling
-Whalen vs Walden
-Edward Lewis 2 days witness Whales vs Walden
-Inventory of the estate of Frederick Fulkerson returned.
-Hairston vs Rickman
-Jacob Lindsay 2 days witness Peter Rickman Jr vs George Hairston
-Mitchell vs Tatum
-Jones vs Yoes Judgement
-Farmer vs Haile same
-Stovall vs Shinault same
-Mills vs Spencer same
-Mitchell vs Jones same
-Mitchell vs Walden same
-James vs Frazier N.P.
-Herndon vs Philips Judgement
-Hairston vs Abington same
-An account of the tax for the year 1791 Thomas Mitchell, Deputy Sheriff of Patrick County, from James Baker of Henry County presented in Court.

-Edward Tatum and Samuel Staples appointed Commissioners in place of Gabriel Penn and Peter Scales (who yesterday were appointed) to take the depositions and examine the Polls on the contest between Joshua Rentfro and John Hughes relative to the election.

PAGE 242

COURT 26 June 1800 present: Edward Tatum, Charles Foster, Gabriel Penn and John Hughes.

-Deed- David Morgan to Alexander Lackey
-Deed- William Sloan to Alexander Lackey
-Deed- William Roberson and wife to Thomas Bondurant
-Deed- George Booth to Samuel Harris
-Deed- Francis Turner and James Turner to Jacob Blackburn
-Deed- Detherick Yoes to Meredith Smith, further proved
-Deed- Jasiel Eckolds to Jacob Adams Sr
-Deed of Trust- Edward Tatum and John Hanby Jr to Dunlap Polock & Co.
-Deed of Trust- John Spencer to Henry L. Biscoe
-Deed of Trust- John Spencer to Dunlap Polock & Company
-Harris Carter 1 day witness H. Koger vs Thomas Bolling
-Robert Lockhart same
-Ordered the Sheriff tax in the Bill of Costs Wilson vs Danger for keeping sundry species of property £3.11.1.
-Augustine Thomas services as processioner allowed 12 days.

Page 242 contd

-Jacob Critz allowed 19½ days for processioning
-Jacob Cummings 31 days for same
-William James Mayo 10 days for same
-Jacob Blackborne 1 day witness William Walden vs James Whalen
-Abel Pedigo same
-Richard Whalen same
-Edward Lewis same
-Noah Parr to serve as Constable in place of F. Fitzgerald.
-Leave is granted Samuel Staples to keep an Ordinary in the town of Taylorsville, William James Mayo his security.
-Hoff vs Pedigo, award to Defendant
-Roland Burnett 4 days witness John Nowlin vs Francis Nowlin
-James Nowlin same
-Eliphaz Shelton 1 day for same
-Mitchell vs Stephens Judgement
-Hughes vs Henderson Judgement
-William Jones appointed surveyor of the road leading from Joshua Rentfros to Eliphaz Sheltons in place of John Fletcher.

PAGE 243

COURT 31 July 1800 present: Francis Turner, Charles Thomas, Edward Tatum and Thomas Whitlock.

-Deed- Jacob Stover to Stephen Maynor
-Deed- William Talbott and David G. Talbott to William Burnett
-Skillern vs Ling dismd
-Thomas Mitchell foreman, William Hancock, John Turner, William Burnett, William Sharp, James Turner, Barnard M. Price, Adrian Anglin, Edward Lewis, John Adams, David Taylor, John Spencer, Sharp Barton, Christopher Long, James Epperson, David Rogers and James Denny to serve as Grand Jury.
-Deed- Beveridge Hughes to William Handy
-Mousure vs Yoes, Elijah Banks Special Bail
-Bill of Sale, Philip Stephens and wife to John Burnett
-Deed- John Jones and wife to William Howell
-Graham vs Bondurant, William Sloan Special Bail, 3 suits with James Harris, Christopher Long and John Breden further Special Bail.
-Morrow vs Lackey dismd

Present: Hamon Critz, Charles Foster, Gabriel Penn, John Hughes, Brett Stovall, Joshua Rentfro, Thomas Whitlock and Peter Scales.

-William Carter, Stephen Lyon and Francis Turner are recommended as fit persons to serve as Sheriff.
-Deed- Jasiel Eckolds to Jacob Adams Sr further proved
-Saunders & Company vs Dehart Judgement
-Deed- Charles Perkins to Samuel Corn further proved
-Deed of Trust- Edward Tatum and John Hanby Jr to Dunlop Pollock & Co further proved
-William James Mayo withdraws his services as Deputy Clerk

Absent: Charles Foster, Joshua Rentfro, Brett Stovall, John Hughes, Gabriel Penn and Hamon Critz.

-Deed- Francis Turner and James Turner to Thomas Blackborne further proved
-Deed- David Morgan to Alexander Lackey further proved
-Deed- David Morgan to William Stone same
-Saunders & Co. vs Chitwood, John Chitwood Special Bail
-Sneed vs Brewer, Judgement granted against Sackville Brewer Jr and William Brewer.
-Anglin vs Brewer
-Deed of Trust- John Spencer to Dunlop Pollock & Co further proved.

PAGE 244

-Deed of Trust- John Spencer to Henry L. Biscoe further proved
-James Turner, Ezariah Denny, James Denny and Jeremiah Denny appeared in Court with John Turner, James Harris and David Harbour their security and are to be of good behavior towards the Citizens of the Commonwealth and to Isaac Collings.
-Peter Bryan allowed 4 days witness Tatum vs Hanby
-Samuel Clark Sr 1 day for same
-Joseph Reynolds 1 day witness Breden vs Morgan
-Mary Alley 1 day witness Blaize vs Amos
-Amos vs Blaize, Plaintiff ruled to give security for costs, he living out of State.
-John Gates 4 days witness Hanby vs Tatum
-Susanah Gates 1 day for same
-Lucy Garrett same
-Eliphaz Shelton 1 day witness Chitwood vs Blankenship
-Isaac Collings to appear for further hearing

COURT 1 August 1800 present: Brett Stovall, John Hughes, Edward Tatum, Francis Turner, Thomas Whitlock, Peter Scales.

-Jacob Adams Sr revokes Power of Attorney given his son William Adams
-Blaize vs Amos contd
-Mary Alley 1 day witness Blaize vs Amos
-Greensville Penn Commissioner of the County presented his accounts and allowed $75.00.
-The Commissioner of land and property tax appeared in Court and qualified to his lists.
-Overseers of the Poor vs Robert Scott for support of a bastard child begotten..Witness did not appear..discharged.
-Stovall vs Roberson, John Hughes Spl Bl
-Hiram Wills to serve as Constable in place of John Jones.

PAGE 245

-Isaac Colling appeared in Court and is to give Bond with security. Taken into custody until the order is complied with.
-Going vs Newman, deposition of John Greenwood and Henry Hart of Stokes County, North Carolina and Nathaniel Scales, Charles Beasley, Noah Scales, James Martin, Thomas Rogers or any three to act as Commissioners for this purpose.
-Lewis vs Jones Judgement
-Gilliam vs Newman, jury sworn: Zachariah Sneed, Sackville Brewer Jr, Humphrey Smith, Joseph Taylor, Eliphaz Shelton, James Haile, John Allen, William Fitzgerald, William Keaton, Joseph Cummings, John Mankin..verdict for Defendant
-Breden vs Morgan redocket
-Blaize vs Amos, Clifton security for costs
-Smith vs Lewis, John Hughes Special Bail
-John Gates 1 day witness Tatum vs Hanby
-Susanah Gates same
-Lucy Garrett same
-Anness Lawson same
-David Rogers 2 days witness Gilliam vs Newman
-Gilliam vs Newman, on a motion of Plaintiff for a new tryall, same was over ruled.
-Miller Easley, 1 day witness Gilliam vs Newman
-Robert Rogers 2 days for same
-John Parr Jr same
-James Lyon Jr same
-Thomas Hornsby same
-Keaton vs Haile and wife Not Guilty
-Joseph Ross 1 day witness Keaton vs Haile
-Patsey Ross same
-George Corn 2 days for same
-Dolley Corn same
-William Fitzgerald same
-Mary Fitzgerald 1 day for same

Page 245 contd

-Sarah Medley 2 days witness Keaton vs Haile
-Archelaus Ward 2 days witness Hanby vs Bennett
-Peter Scales 2 days witness Tatum vs Smith
-William Deal Jr 7 days witness Keaton vs Haile
-Mary Lemmon 3 days for same
-Joseph Taylor 2 days 18 miles witness White vs Tatum
-Susanah Carter 2 days for same

PAGE 246

COURT 2 July 1800 present: Jonathan Hanby, Edward Tatum, John Hughes and Joshua Rentfro

-Smith vs Poteet and others, take deposition of James White, George McNutt??, John White, John Lavender, John Od--- or any three to take deposition of Ezekiel McPeak for the Defendant.
-Deed- Miller Easley to Joshua Rentfro
-Going vs Newman contd
-Wilson Sr vs Danger, jury sworn: Humphrey Smith, Sackville Brewer Jr, Nathaniel Smith, William Smith, Archelaus Hughes, John Hanby, Eliphaz Shelton, John Mankin, David Hanby, Thomas Hornsby, William Witt and Joseph Taylor..verdict returned for Pltf.
-Calaway & Ward vs Roberson
-Danger vs D. Martindill dismd
-Danger vs J. Martindill same
-White vs Tatum contd
-Mousure vs Yoes contd
-John Gates allowed 1 day witness Hanby vs Tatum
-Susanah Gates same
-Joseph Taylor allowed 1 day witness White vs Tatum
-Sackville Brewer Jr 3 days for same
-Lucy Garrett 1 day witness Hanby vs Tatum
-Peter Bryant 2 days for same
-John Breden Jr 3 days witness Smith vs Tatum
-George Corn 1 day witness Haile vs Keaton
-Dolley Corn same
-Jesse Tatum Sr, 7 days witness Fagin vs Commonwealth
-Joseph Ross 1 day witness Keaton vs Haile
-Patsey Ross same
-David Hanby 3 days witness White vs Tatum
-Susanah Carter 1 day for same
-Mary Fitzgerald 1 day witness Haile vs Keaton
-William Deal 1 day witness Tatum vs Smith
-Sarah Medley 1 day witness Haile vs Keaton
-Anness Lawson 1 day witness Tatum vs Hanby
-Malichi Cummings 2 days witness Keaton vs Haile
-Mary Lemmons 1 day for same
-Richard Davidson 4 days witness Tatum vs Smith
-Joseph Keaton 5 days witness Keaton vs Haile
-Judith Keaton same
-John Mankin 2 days witness Fagin vs Commonwealth
-Joshua Rentfro 4 days witness Keaton vs Haile
-Archelaus Taylor 2 days witness Wilson Sr vs Danger

PAGE 247

-John Wilson 2 days witness Jonathany Hanby vs Fagin
-Daniel Martindill 6 days witness Wilson vs Danger
-John Bennett 3 days witness Fagin vs Hanby
-Laughlin Fagin 3 days witness Bennett vs Hanby
-Mary Fagin 3 days witness Tatum vs Hanby
-Archelaus witness Hanby vs Fagin

-Isaac Collings appeared in Court with Jesse Corn and Joseph Going as his security. To be of good behavior for 12 months 1 day.
-Deed- Isaac Collings to Mary Vaughan
-Deed of Trust- Isaac Collings to Jesse Corn and Joseph Goings

Page 247 contd

-Adams vs Keaton, Defendant to pay costs

COURT 28 August 1800 present: Joshua Rentfro, Edward Tatum, Samuel Packwood, Brett Stovall, Charles Foster.

--Hairston vs Devonshire contd
-Smith vs McNanney contd
-Nowlin for the benefit of Saunders & Co vs Nowlin
-Hannah vs Manning contd
-Koger vs Bolling contd
-Harris Carter 3 days witness Koger vs Bolling
-Robert Lockhart 3 days for same
-Whalen vs Walden contd
-Jacob Blackborne 1 day witness William Walden vs Whalen
-Richard Whalen 1 day for same
-Eliphaz Shelton 1 day witness John Nowlin vs Francis Nowlin
-Abel Pedigo 1 day witness William Walden vs James Whalen
-Hairston vs Rickman contd
-Heath vs Mayner contd
-Mitchell vs Tatum contd
-Wade vs Spencer Judgement
-Saunders vs Chitwood contd
-Rowan & Scott vs Ross contd
-Banks vs Turner Judgement
-James Harris 1 day witness Roland Lee vs Thomas Blackborne

PAGE 248

-Penn & Clark vs Fry contd
-Rowan & Scott vs Harris contd
-Mitchell assignee vs Going N.P.
-same vs Lewis Judgement
-same vs Franzier same
-same vs William Haile same
-same vs Hubbard same
-same vs Frans same
-same vs Joseph Keaton same
-same vs Benjamin Haile N.P.
-Dillen vs Hodges N.P.
-John Dalton qualified as Deputy Sheriff under William Carter.
-Edward Lewis 1 day witness Whalen vs Walden
-Bill of Sale- John Spencer to Brett Stovall
-Deed- William Turman to ----Ferguson
-Staples vs Blackborne, award to Defendant
-Smith vs Ross N.P.
-Smith vs Lewis contd
-Smith vs Price contd
-Hairston vs Abington Judgement
-William Harris 1 day witness Roland Lee vs Thomas Blackborne
-Pers--- vs Brewer Jr Judgement
-Samuel Scritchfield appointed surveyor of the road from the top of Bull Mountain to Gossetts bounds in place of Ignatious-----..
-James Turner, John Breden Jr, William Sloan and William Fuson or any three of them to view a way for a road from James Dennys to the Carolina line on the direction to the head of Read Island.
-Robert Sharp appointed surveyor of the road in place of George Lackey from the top of Bull Mountain to Foleys.
-George Lackey appointed surveyor of the road from the forks of the road by said Lackeys to the Sycamore Road.
-Overseers of the Poor on behalf of Jane Barton vs David Rogers on a recognizence for support of a bastard child of said Jane Barton, on consideration thereof, Judgement for the sum of five pounds.
-Samuel Packwood 1 day witness Smith vs McNanney
-James Nowlin 1 day witness Francis Nowlin vs John Nowlin
-Samuel Staples appointed Jailor in place of Benjamin Philpott

JUSTICES of Patrick County, Virginia with page references when they served in that capacity.

James Armstrong 2,5,7,8,22,25,28,34,35,37,39,46,65,71,
William Banks 2,3,5,11,12,13,14,16,18,28,37,44,49,55,57,68,70,71,72,74,76,77,80,86,88,93,94,97,100,102,109,110,120,122,132,139,147,150,158,168,170,172,177,179,194,206,211,217,219,221,226
John Breden Jr., 42,46,48,49,51,55,57,60,66,68,70,77,80,81,83,84,85,87,88,90,92,94,127,134,136,138,146,161,175
Daniel Carlin 2,181
William Carter 2,5,7,8,9,11,16,21,22,23,24,28,30,33,35,36,37,42,55,62,71,83,87,94,106,108,120,125,158,161,165,168,181,187,194,195,202,211,223
Samuel Clark 2,3,7,8,9,11,12,14,17,18,21,22,23,28,33,34,36,44,49,51,52,55,57,60,62,66,68,80,88,92,94,99,102,107,108,109,110,115,117,120,132,135,145,147,154,157,161,162,165,168,169,170,194
Hamon Critz, Jr., 51,55,74,84,86,90,113,115,117,119,120,132,134,139,165,174,175,186,191,194,202,205,208,210,214,217,221,223,224,226,230,233,239,240,241,243
Charles Foster 2,5,8,21,22,23,25,33,37,57,60,70,71,77,80,90,95,97, 104,107,121,122,125, 142,143,145,150,152,158,164,168,178,179,181,184,186,187,189,208,216,217,221,227,228,230,234,236,242,243,247
Jonathan Hanby 2,8,13,30,33,36,62,63,64,65,86,87,93,94,101,113,184,194,202,205,217,233,240,246
Archelaus Hughes 9,14,33,34,35,36,39,42,44,63,64,65,66,70,71,76,80,811,83,88,90,92,93,94,97,100,102,106,107,108,109,110,113,114,121,122,124,127,128,132,134,135,
John Hughes 175,177,178,179,181,184,194,198,202,203,210,213,214,216,217,219,221,226,227,228,233,239,240,242,243,244,246
James Lyon 2,3,7,8,9,11,12,13,14,16,17,18,21,22,24,28,30,33,34,35,37,41,46,49,52,55,59,62,63,64,65,66,68,81,86,87,89,90,92,94,101,106,108,110,112,113,114,117,118,120,121,124,125,127,128,131,134
Stephen Lyon 2,8,12,30,35,36,41,42,49,52,7994,99,113,115,120,124,131,134,179,194,195,198
James Lyon (add) 139,143,145,146,148,154,161,162,165,166,167,168,169,170,172,174,240
Samuel Packwood 94,136,152,169,174,201,221,247
Abraham Penn 2,8,16,17,18,22,23,24,25,28,33,36,41,46,48,49,52,55,57,59,60,63,64,65,76,77,79,92,95,97,99,104,108,114,118,119,136,152,166,167,168,172,186,187,201,208,221,236,238
Gabriel Penn87,93,95,97,99,104,106,107,122,136,142,150,152,221,226,227,231,233,238,242,243
George Penn Jr., 39,57,59,62,65,66,69,72,74,79,121,146,164,167,168,172,178,186,194,195,208,216,217,221,223,236
Joshua Rentfro 127,132,133,134,135,136,137,139,145,147,154,158,161,162,165,166,168,169,174,178,181,186,189,191,194,201,202,208,210,216,217,218,219,221,223,228,243,246,247
Munford Smith 80,94,113,128,167,168
Brett Stovall 39,51,55,64,65,72,74,77,80,83,84,85,94,97,102,106,115,118,119,120,122,124,130,131,133,134,136,143,164,165,172,174,177,178,181,192,194,195,198,199,205,206,210,211,213,214,216,221,224,228,230,243,244,247
Joseph Stovall 41,60,71,81,84,94,95,112,113,134,162,165,169,170,172,175,177,178,194,199,206,210,216,217,221,223,231,233,238,240,241
Edward Tatum46,49,55,59,60,62,64,65,79,84,85,86,87,88,101,104,106,107,108,110,113,114,120,125,130,132,133,134,135,146,148,152,155,157,161,165,168,169,194,199,201,202,203,208,214,217,218,219,221,224,226,227,228,230,231,234,238,239,241,242,243,244,246,247
PeterScales 202,203,205,208,213,214,216,243,244
Charles Thomas 42,48,51,52,55,65,71,74,77,84,85,93,94,100,104,107,112,113,114,120,121,125,133,134,135,137,142,148,150,152,157,158,162,164,166,169,189,194,206,210,21 7,218,221,223,228,230,231,234,236,239,240,243
Francis Turner 2,5,7,8,9,13,14,17,18,22,23,24,25,30,34,35,37,39,41,44,48,49,60,70,71,72,81,88,90,100,102,104,109,110,112,117,118,119,120,121,122,128,130,133,134,135,138,142,143,148,150,155,157,158,164,167,168,169,184,186,189,191,194,198,199,203,210,211,216,218,223,224,234,243,244
Thomas Whitlock 128,130, 147,243,244

INDEX

www.ingramcontent.com/pod-product-compliance
Lightning Source LLC
Chambersburg PA
CBHW021833020426
42334CB00014B/614

* 9 7 8 0 8 9 3 0 8 4 2 7 1 *